Brunschwig & Fils® UP CLOSE

Brunschwig & Fils UP CLOSE

FROM GRAND ROOMS TO YOUR ROOMS

MURRAY DOUGLAS AND CHIPPY IRVINE

BULFINCH PRESS

New York • Boston

Bulfinch Press

Time Warner Book Group
1271 Avenue of the Americas
New York, NY 10020
Visit our Web site at www.bulfinchpress.com

FIRST EDITION

Second Printing, 2006

Library of Congress Cataloging-in-Publication Data

Douglas, Murray.
    Brunschwig & Fils up close : from grand rooms to your rooms / Murray Douglas and Chippy Irvine.—1st ed.
        p. cm.
    Includes bibliographical references and indexes.
    ISBN 0-8212-2859-5
    1. Brunschwig & fils. 2. Textile fabrics—History—20th century. 3. Textile fabrics in interior decoration.
 I. Irvine, Chippy. II. Title.

    NK8998.B76D684 2440
    746'.09747'1—dc22   2004008730

Design by Joel Avirom, Jason Snyder, and Meghan Day Healey

Printed in Singapore

This book is dedicated to interior designers all over the world—
for whom Brunschwig evolved and without whom Brunschwig would not exist.

Contents

M DOUGLAS '04

Introduction

With the success of *Brunschwig & Fils Style,* now in its fourth printing, we felt the need for a companion book. Many designers have told us how they use *Brunschwig & Fils Style* as a resource for discovering and identifying decorative products. From Australia—which now has two Brunschwig & Fils showrooms—designer Lill Reid tells us, "I still refer to that book, though I sometimes drive the people in the showroom mad by wanting discontinued fabric!"

In the past ten years many developments and innovations have taken place within the Brunschwig & Fils company. The world has also changed considerably since the first book was conceived. Interior decoration itself has undergone transformations, due to what we superficially call "trends" but which really are serious echoes of shifts in technology, politics, economics, and society. We have been through black-brown-beige simplification to superexpensive minimalism and back again to long-lasting, personal, traditional interiors—and many more changes still lie ahead.

What does not alter is the continuous need for creativity and imagination. Designers, whether of complete interiors or of the building blocks needed for interiors—the wall coverings, carpets, fabric, and furnishings—must be open to ideas and able to combine these ideas to produce beautiful and appropriate living spaces.

I remember how well my aunt Zelina Brunschwig was able to harness and foster many ideas, seemingly at the spur of the moment. When asked by a customer, "But what should I do with this fabric?" Mrs. B. would describe a room that she had "just seen" in her head with a favorite Brunschwig & Fils fabric used as the "theme," extemporize about the treatment of the walls, the Aubusson rug, the elegant chaise longue, the lamps on the skirted table, the mirrored paneled screen, the console, the cushions, and the flowers. The picture she painted was so real and visible to the designer that he or she could go away with a concrete idea or concept for the client. In this book Chippy and I have endeavored to present the creativity of our talented designers to stimulate how you think about your challenges and find inspiration using our products in contemporary ways. Mrs. B.'s kind of imagination—backed by continually improving business systems—is the touchstone of Brunschwig & Fils to this day.

Murray Douglas

Part One
Historical Inspiration

MUSÉE DE L'IMPRESSION ▓ SUR ÉTOFFES
MULHOUSE

BRUNSCHWIG & FILS

Un éditeur new-yorkais interprète la culture textile européenne

6 MAI 2003
22 FEVRIER 2004

Sièges KUSTER André & fils - Bertrand KLEIN Antiquités - TENDANCIEL à HABSHEIM

Caves de TURCKHEIM - Avec la participation d'Isabelle de BORCHGRAVE

*Ouvert tous les jours de 10h à 12h et de 14h à 18h sauf le lundi du 2 Mai au 30 septembre

*Ouvert tous les jours de 10h à 12h et de 14h à 18h sauf le lundi et Mardi du 1er Octobre au 30 Avril

14, RUE JEAN-JACQUES HENNER - BP 1468 | F 68072 MULHOUSE CEDEX | TÉL. : 03 89 46 83 00 / FAX : 03 89 46 83 10

K'CEREIA 03 89 43 51 49

1

The Fabric of Our Lives
Textile Techniques

Early Fabric Techniques Brunschwig & Fils has been associated for many years with its vast range of more than twenty thousand luxurious fabrics. Today, its many other products include wallpaper, trimmings, upholstered furniture, tables, and lighting, but Brunschwig & Fils' tradition remains inextricably identified with high-quality decorative textiles from all over the world.

For thousands of years, artisans have woven textiles using natural materials—hemp (which has been used for at least twenty-five thousand years), linen, wool, cotton, and even bark and nuts. In the beginning weaving was a plain over-and-under pattern, but we now know that tapestry and brocading techniques have been around since 3000 BC. Egyptian mummies were wrapped in woven linen, sometimes dyed using madder, an ancient red made from the roots of the madder plant, which is found throughout Europe and Asia. Indigo, a cold-bath dye made from a shrubby plant found in India, was another early discovery.

Gradually, ingenuity and creativity entered the process. Most early fabric techniques began in Asia. Five thousand years ago, garments of dyed-and-patterned cotton were being produced in the Indus Valley. The burial sites of four-thousand-year-old mummies in Chinese Turkestan revealed remarkably well preserved, colorful, woolen textiles. As the textile trade

PREVIOUS SPREAD
A wallpaper border named after Walt Whitman's poem *Leaves of Grass*.

OPPOSITE
This poster illustrates the 2003 exhibition of Brunschwig & Fils' fine textiles at the Musée de l'Impression sur Étoffes in Mulhouse. The show was a special honor for the now-American-based firm because Mulhouse, in Alsace, France, is known as a cradle of French textile production.

developed from east to west, ancient Rome's wealthiest citizens became infatuated by lightweight, glistening silk carried overland from China along the fabled Silk Road.

All these wondrous handmade stuffs took months—even years—to produce, and they were often manufactured under the patronage of local temples. As textiles were increasingly traded over the vast Asian continent, making their way to the Middle East and thence to Europe, manufacturing techniques spread, mutated, and were enhanced and adapted to different climates, resources, and tastes.

The weaving of an ikat—from a Malay word—required certain threads of the warp to be tied in bundles to "resist" color from penetrating when it was dipped in dye. The bundles were then untied, and the process repeated—over and over again using other threads and colors—until a complex design was achieved. Then the fabric was woven, producing a design that was the same on both sides. Through overland trade, the technique spread. The Japanese developed double ikats with warp and weft threads tied and dyed, but these were possible only in small lengths—large enough, say, for a kimono. In Afghanistan, ikat warp-dyeing became renowned and had a vigorous ethnic quality, a look that is popular for today's casual life, though now such effects are achieved by surface printing. The French, always aiming at refinement, developed warp-dyed techniques (which they called *chinés*) to produce very different, delicate, and expensive silks.

Batiks from Java were obtained by wax-resist methods. *Bandhani* work (mentioned in writings as early as the seventh century) is a form of tie- or knot-dyeing using wax thread, with fine examples coming from Gujarat and Rajasthan, in India. Our word *bandanna* derives from it.

OPPOSITE

This hall, designed by Dottebob Andes, of Sanderling Interiors, in Haverford, Pennsylvania, is made particularly arresting by the use of *Majorca Ikat,* a printed design inspired by early warp-dyed textile techniques. The chair seats feature *Soligny.*

Kalamkari   When Genghis Khan was in power, weaving techniques spread by land to many parts of his domain, from Iran to Central Asia and Mongolia and from China to as far west as Samarqand. It wasn't until the great Dutch, Portuguese, English, Danish, and French trading companies of Europe developed efficient sea routes to India in the sixteenth and seventeenth centuries that trade accelerated with Asia. The West set out after the lucrative spice trade, but in the meantime discovered hand-painted, colorful, washable cotton fabrics that had been made in India for centuries. According to Sabrina Parashar, writing for *Indian Women Online,* "The Coromandel Coast of India was historically the source of some of the most beautifully colored and delicately worked cotton fabrics. Here mordants, resists, and brushes or pens were traditionally applied and used to produce figurative and floral designs of great fineness."

These decorated fabrics were known in India as *kalamkari* (sometimes *qalamkari*): *kalam* being Persian for "pen," and *kari* meaning "work." The Portuguese, the first to import them, called them *pintado;* the French called them *indiennes* (now also an American term, used by Brunschwig & Fils); and the English called them chintz, from the Sanskrit word *chitra.* Though frequently referred to as "painted" cottons, many were decorated using a form of pen—a stick of bamboo or date palm given a tapered point with a one-inch slit like an outsize nib, above which was a ball of wool used as a reservoir for dye. Woodblocks were employed for a form of printing in seventeenth-century India, but only for outlines. The details were filled in with pens or brushes; printing was considered inferior. Centers for the finest work were Masulipatnam, which had historic Persian links and showed Muslim-influenced designs; and Srikalahasti, which showed Hindu influences.

Kalamkari textiles were used mainly for curtains, bed covers, and upholstery and occasionally for clothing. Design motifs included the familiar cone motif found in what we often call a paisley design; verses from the Koran; the mihrab, or arch, motif; and figures with rounded bodies, bold expressive eyes, and detailed costumes and jewelry. But all of these designs seem to have been inspired by one particular theme based on nature—the tree of life.

OPPOSITE

New York designer Gary Crain used a printed indienne called *Ceylon* on the walls, curtains, and upholstery of this porch for the Southampton showhouse 2001 at the Villa Maria, Southampton, New York.

ABOVE

Using *Karikal* palampore cotton print—and its accompanying stripe and rock garden—Liz Mitchell of Marblehead, Massachusetts, created this bedroom vignette.

OPPOSITE

Brunschwig's spring 2003 collection showed a new version of the palampore tree-of-life design. In a sketch freelance stylist Bill Walter proposed uses of *Karikal* for the brochure. Four *Karikal* designs were derived from a hand-penned 1720 documentary palampore: a stripe (from the border), a rock garden (from the base), a porcelain motif, plus the complete bedspread-size panel.

The Tree of Life

Colonel Brunschwig's American wife, Zelina (Mrs. B.), collected documentary textiles into the Brunschwig Archive. The colonel's father's archival collection had been moved from Paris to New York during World War II and was added to Mrs. B.'s growing textile library. Ever curious about historic designs, she asked museum curators, "Why are there no printed textiles before the seventeenth and eighteenth centuries?" In the answer she discovered that the grandfather of printed designs was the tree of life *(le grand arbre),* with a wide, decorative border penned or painted onto plain-weave, unbleached cotton palampores, or bed cover–size pieces. This design had been formalized in India by the seventeenth century—and probably before. It included rocky or mossy ground from which grew a sinuous trunk, spreading to branches, leaves,

and fantastic flowers, with birds perched or flitting through them. Endless variations were possible, depending on the imagination and skill of the artist.

Europeans were attracted to these exotic cottons, which were comfortable to wear and could be washed without losing their colors. Trade of these fabrics reached a peak in the last quarter of the seventeenth century. To help answer Mrs. B.'s question, at least two seventeenth-century Indian palampores made their way to America. One was found at Gunston Hall. The second was unearthed when Florence Montgomery, then the curator of textiles at the Winterthur Estate in Delaware, discovered some chair-seat coverings that had been recycled from a full-size palampore. The fact that Europeans and Americans used chairs (not a normal piece of Indian furniture) meant that these colorful designs were needed by the West in smaller repeats. Western demands began to influence Indian designs. Exported indiennes began to be seen with white grounds rather than Indian purple or red ones, flowers became less outrageously exotic, and repeats became smaller.

By the beginning of the eighteenth century, the *kalamkari* trade began to dwindle as the secrets of their manufacture leaked out—especially the formulas of the various mordants needed to fix the colors. The French, followed by the rest of Europe, began to produce their own colorfast cottons, adapting them to their preferred naturalistic style—real-looking flowers and leaves—spurred on by the fashionable study of nature and scientific discoveries.

The Printed Calico Quarrel   Some countries banned the

importation and manufacture of *kalamkari* cloth. France, fearing the Indian cloth would cut into French-produced luxury woven goods, velvets, and brocaded silks, passed two edicts and eighty decrees between 1686 and 1756—which were frequently flouted. The French port city Marseilles, which was an on-again, off-again free port, traded and produced indiennes that inspired the distinctive Provençal prints we know today. Genoa, then an independent city-state, became wealthy as a free port that traded Indian fabric, even producing its own distinctive cotton shawls known as *mezzari,* or *voiles de Gênes,* which used tree-of-life motifs in horizontal designs.

England, Holland, Switzerland, and some areas around the Mediterranean soon lifted their bans on importing and manufacturing printed textiles. This led them to more advanced manufacturing technologies while the French were still embroiled in the banning of printed-cloth manufacturing—known as the Printed Calico Quarrel (though smuggling and small-time printing continued surreptitiously). The lure of fashion is difficult to suppress, and the practicalities of washable, hard-wearing, and inexpensive fabric could no longer be denied. By the time the ban was lifted in France, many skilled Huguenot textile craftsmen had been banished for religious reasons. France had to turn to foreigners to acquaint them with the latest dyeing and printing methods.

France's best-known fabric printing factory was founded by a "foreigner"—German-born, Swiss-trained genius Christophe-Philippe Oberkampf, who settled near Versailles at Jouy-en-Josas. The manufactory survived only from 1760 to 1844 but produced wonderful, high-quality printed textiles—designs still in demand today. The name toile de Jouy is now generic. (See p. 19.)

Gaya, an indienne from the spring 2004 collection, was based on a document found at the Château de Grancey, near Dijon. It is an example of printed calico with a lot of light-colored ground put into repeats for the European market, rather than showing a complete, sinuous tree of life.

Advances in Fabric Printing
Innovations in fabric printing continued throughout the late eighteenth and nineteenth centuries, moving from slow and cumbersome block printing to copper-plate printing to an early form of roller printing (when the flat copper plate became a cylindrical roller). Fabric was placed on rollers and stretched, then burnished with an agate stone to give a polished effect—the forerunner of a calendered, or glazed, technique.

The dyeing and printing of fabrics had always been achieved using animal- and vegetable-derived dyes. Crimson, for instance, was obtained from the cochineal beetle (also used for food dye in England until the 1940s), but seventeen thousand tiny insects were needed to make one ounce of dyestuff. Dyeing cloth had always been a messy and particularly smelly business. Great quantities of cow dung (elephant dung in India) were needed as a mordant at the Jouy manufactory. In the middle of the nineteenth century, a breakthrough took place with the discovery of chemical dyes. According to Simon Garfield, author of *Mauve: How One Man Invented a Color That Changed the World,* in 1856 an eighteen-year-old English chemistry student named William Perkin discovered a black sludge that turned cloth a "strangely beautiful" soft purple. A way to mass-produce color was finally found. Prior to that time, purple (made from the glandular mucus of mollusks) was prohibitively expensive and known as Tyrian, or royal, purple. Perkin's discovery was of colorfast aniline dyes derived from coal tar. His mauve-colored dye made him famous when Queen Victoria wore a dress in that shade at her daughter's wedding, in 1858. That same year it was taken up by fashion-obsessed Empress Eugénie, known for announcing, "Worth and I rule Paris." She decided that the new mauve exactly matched her eyes.

Coal-tar derivatives are now used in many products, from saccharine to chemotherapy, as well as in most of our present-day dyes.

The twentieth century brought more innovations. Although roller printing produced multicolored patterns quickly, and thus inexpensively, designers sought a technique that imitated block printing and the subtle colorations that came with overprinting. Building on the idea of Japanese stencils, a method called silk-screen printing came to the fore in the 1930s and was refined over fifty years until hand-printed silk screens could produce block-printed effects—especially the distinctive overprinted effects. The screens are now made of Dacron, not silk.

Today, rotary screen printing produces large quantities with up to twenty-five colors in a timely fashion—but for truly subtle designs, hand screen printing is preferable to machine-printed products.

Once screen printing became available, many printed designs from the past were revived. Printed reproductions of brocaded silks and lampas designs were made possible on today's more-favored cotton and linen. Brunschwig made eloquent use of its archival material to revive patterns that were too expensive to weave and, with fresh color, reintroduced lost designs to a newly awakened audience.

New Old Designs
Among the favorite designs then and now are *Fontainebleau, Les Perdrix, Campanula, Pillement, Couronne Imperiale, Le Lac, Arbre Japonais, Sybilla, Tournier Rose,* and *Les Roseaux Tropicaux.* The last is such a favorite that it was translated into wallpaper, as seen in Lannie Cornett's dining room on page 15. His philosophy, as told to Murray Douglas, runs: "Emerson said, 'Owning a home is a lifetime achievement. One must take great care to nurture and refine it.' That's why I love Brunschwig & Fils. Interiors must look like they have evolved. Nothing shouts, but it looks acquired over time, like classic European homes."

Though myriad designs have appeared since the invention of fabric printing, the grandfather of them all, the tree of life, remains an inspiration and is still in demand. *La Portugaise,* one of Brunschwig's best-loved prints, is a descendant of indienne designs. It is a nineteenth-century adaptation made up from the borders of a palampore formed into stripes. Its name, *La Portugaise,* comes from the heavy trading between India and Portugal, especially in Goa, once a Portuguese colony.

Occasionally, woven fabrics are inspired by prints. *Kandahar* is a popular offspring of the tree of life—probably

OVERLEAF LEFT
Austrian architect and designer Josef Frank (1885–1967) was inspired by the tree of life in his mid-twentieth-century fabric design *Vegetable Tree,* now sold in the United States at Brunschwig & Fils.

OVERLEAF RIGHT
Chicago and New York decorator Lannie Cornett designed the dining room shown in this vignette using *Les Roseaux Tropicaux* (bulrushes). This design is based on a French document and exists as both wallpaper and fabric.

designed in the nineteenth century in Oberkampf's Jouy factory because the documentary design was given to a French fabric manufacturer by Oberkampf's great-great-great-granddaughter. This printed tree of life–inspired design was adapted into a woven damask with a slightly smaller repeat so it could work for today's furniture, for which the original fifty-five-inch repeat would have been too big. The designers at Brunschwig's Studio are especially interested in developing tree of life–inspired damasks from the Archive because they give an organic and exhilarating effect of growing upward, making them immediately dynamic. (See *Talavera* on p. 215, for the mention of an example of a wallpaper inspiring a woven fabric; *Sultan of Gujarat* for an antique woven rug inspiring a print on p. 201; and *Le Lac* on p. 35, for an example of a brocaded *woven* fabric inspiring a *print.*)

Every few years a new version of the tree of life shows up in a Brunschwig collection, complete with subsidiary designs such as stripes formed from the borders and overall patterns formed from the stylized ground cover (see Dennis Rolland's use of *Nanou Rockery* on p. 157). Tree-of-life designs include the classic *Grand Genois* (imported from France); *Palampore,* introduced in 1993 and adapted from a document at the Royal Ontario Museum, in Toronto; *Karikal* in the 2003 collection (see Liz Mitchell's use of it on p. 8); and a striking mid-twentieth-century series of tree-of-life designs by the Austrian architect and designer Josef Frank, who gave his work a particularly 1940s flavor. He even made a fabric design based on a map of Manhattan that has been used with great flair in several New York hotels. His fabrics are now sold by Brunschwig in the United States. Especially colorful and eye-catching is his witty *Vegetable Tree.*

OPPOSITE

In this New Jersey foyer, Carl D'Aquino of D'Aquino/Monaco used *Malabar Coast* in imperial blue, a woven design based on the printed design of *Kandahar.* The curtains are trimmed with lapis-colored moss fringe. (See p. 75 for another photograph of this house.)

2

Fine Lines
The ABCs of Toile

There is a growing public awareness of toiles—those finely drawn, monotone prints usually showing a theme or story of some sort. Their popularity today comes because they are easy to live with: unobtrusive, of a single color, and unpretentious from a distance; but, as you draw close, something—a picture or some discernible content—always causes the eye to linger. Toiles are so popular that even household and garden catalogs frequently show simplified versions of them on tablecloths, napkins, aprons, and bed linen.

When Murray Douglas, who frequently lectures on the decorative arts, gives her talk called "The ABCs of Toile de Jouy," she describes the first time she saw toile used the French way—en suite—at the Musée des Arts Décoratifs, where a monotone toile was used on walls, curtains, and as a tablecloth. Fabric would be fixed to a wood frame on the wall over a layer of flannel, and a braid or some form of trimming would cover the nails or staples. Later, fabrics were sometimes printed on firm canvas or backed with paper to achieve a wall covering, but gradually it became obvious that there was a need to print toile wallpapers—though you can only guarantee an absolutely perfect match if you use the same fabric for curtains, upholstery, and walls.

The word *toile* in French means plain, woven cotton. The interior-design community outside France says toile de Jouy when referring to any printed monotone engraved designs. The most famous toiles came from the factory at Jouy-en-Josas (which also produced many multicolored, block-printed fabrics as well). Other French

OPPOSITE

This attic dressing room was designed by New York designer Tonin MacCallum for a Kips Bay showhouse. With its chaise, blue satin pajamas, and red slippers, it has an intriguingly tousled, sexy look. The black-and-white toile is *Bird and Thistle,* from a Winterthur Estate document, and it has been given a snappy bandbox finish with *Dempsey* red tape.

Tucson, Arizona, designer Christy Martin, working for Studio Encanto, designed a bedroom in Toledo, Ohio, using green-on-white *Bromley Hall* toile and border en suite, in the classic manner, on both walls and furnishings.

factories, such as those in Nantes, produced less finely drawn monotone toiles (see pp. 182–183 for Yves Taralon's bedroom using a *toile de Nantes*). The tale of toile, nevertheless, is linked with Christophe-Philippe Oberkampf and the manufactory of Jouy-en-Josas, and toile de Jouy has become a general term.

Because the French were embroiled in their internal Printed Calico Quarrel mentioned in the previous chapter, the Irish (as early as 1760), English, Swiss, and some European countries around the Mediterranean leaped ahead of the French, technically, in the colorfast printing of these distinctive monotone copper plate or plate prints, as they were called in the English-speaking mills. These finely drawn prints were an offshoot of the thriving copper-plate engraving on paper industry, which influenced many aspects of design, including ceramics such as Liverpool Transfer ware. Copper-plate-printed fabric was quicker to produce and, therefore, less expensive than multicolored designs, and the results appealed to a wide public. However, when the French ban on printing on cotton was lifted, things changed. Oberkampf had been to English factories and brought back some designs. At first the French copper-plate prints were influenced by English designs, mostly of birds and flowers. But soon the French excelled with their brilliant print designers—Jean-Baptiste Huet, in particular—and their sophisticated ideas. Many of these were inspired and borrowed from fine artists such as Claude Lorrain, Nicolas Lancret, François Boucher, and engraver and artist Jean-Baptiste Pillement, who was

Brunschwig's director of advertising and public relations, Robert Raymond (seen here), had the walls of his New York office upholstered with blue *Cathay* toile in the approved way—using a wood frame fitted to the wall with flannel padding under the toile fabric. A nice touch is making the narrow border from the toile into a flat binding to cover the edges. Super-bright sunshine on that side of the building at certain times of the day requires blinds, which also match. (See other uses of *Cathay* in William/Wayne's living room on p. 38 and in a New Zealand hall on p. 133.)

Greenville, South Carolina, decorator Barbara
Southerland designed this formal drawing
room for a Federal house, Beverly Hall, in
Edenton, North Carolina, using *Four Seasons*
toile for the curtains, draperies, and swags
hung from antique, wood-carved pelmets.
Over the years several versions of this
particular toile have been created, as it has an
especially attractive flowing design scheme.

a superb decorative stylist. Distinguished animated and genre designs were produced that are still desirable today.

One well-known French-printed monotone toile of the late eighteenth century was called *Les travaux de la manufacture* (The activities of the factory). It depicts meticulously drawn vignettes of the whole printing process as a cottage industry, illustrated with romantic bucolic settings, rustic branches, and vegetation in a style that might have delighted Marie Antoinette, with her passion for all things pastoral and "simple." The scenes on the toile include bundles of woven cloth brought from individual cottages to be washed in the river and set out to dry and then beaten; cloth to be printed using blocks full of dye tapped with a mallet to transfer the color laid out on tables; fabric being dipped in the dung bath to fix the dye; and material staked out to dry or hung from the eaves of a three-story building.

Copper-plate printing was finer and more mechanized than cumbersome woodblock printing. Plates, however, sometimes became worn after time and caused printing problems. Some of the original late-eighteenth-century plates were still in use until the mid twentieth century, but they produced narrow fabric with dye-smudged edges where the metal had worn away. When seamed together, the design formed a messy channel of color.

Seaming was not always carried out correctly, even in the early usage of toile. Because the fabric was expensive, many upholsterers and seamstresses were loath to waste good material on matching seams correctly. This has led to the quirkiness of the owners of certain historic houses wanting to duplicate the mismatched-seam effect when refurbishing a room!

About 1790, copper cylindrical rollers came into use, speeding up the process because they could print continuously. Toiles printed by rollers can often be identified because the repeats are smaller and less expanse of white background exists. As with the colorful indiennes, pure white backgrounds had been much valued on toiles. By the beginning of the early nineteenth century, designs started to shift to bolder neoclassical motifs such as diamond lozenges, ovals, and round cameos framing Grecian figures, cupids, sphinxes, and pyramids in sepia and blue set on darkened, patterned, or etched-looking

grounds. *Kininvie,* a Brunschwig favorite, is an early, multicolored, classic revival of a copper-plate design from England, about 1789–90. Many neoclassic designs have survived into the twenty-first century—such as *Les Sphinx Médaillons*—and are still in demand. The early rollers produced narrow goods, approximately thirty-one inches wide. Big, and expensive to make, many rollers lasted well into the twentieth century, though most of the original copper plates were melted down in 1914 for munitions in the First World War.

With the gradual perfecting of screen printing from the 1930s on, the finest of "fine lines" of toile are now produced by this method. In some cases as screens were made, a tendency to draw far more

Designer Linda Axe of LVL Enterprises, Grosse Pointe, MI, designed this guest bedroom for the Junior League 2002 Showhouse using carnelian-on-cream *Kininvie* as fabric and wallpaper. An English design (despite the Scottish name), *Kininvie*'s pattern comes from an early, multicolored toile from about 1789–90. The room also features a *Hortense* day bed and red *Trapunto* matelassé. The watercolor is by Murray Douglas. (*Kininvie* can also be seen in Jo Archibald's bedroom on p. 131.)

freely than before occurred, so that the fine, copper-plate-engraved effect was discarded in favor of a looser, more-painterly line.

We take black-and-white toiles for granted today, but this coloring came into fashion only in the mid twentieth century. American designer Melanie Kahane, who became well known in the 1950s and 1960s, created a sensation when she used a black-and-white toile with bright orange furniture.

3

Chinoiserie
The Lure of the East

Murray Douglas's inspiring lecture entitled "Chinoiserie, The Lure of the East" shows (through rare slides) and tells (through probing research) how chinoiserie evolved and why it has captivated the imagination of Europeans and Americans for three hundred years.

Until the seventeenth century, few Westerners had actually seen China. This vast country had been known since Roman times as the source of the irresistible fabric silk, but by the third century AD, barbarian tribes had rendered the Silk Route insecure. In the early thirteenth century Genghis Khan unified the Mongols and conquered the lands between China and the Caspian Sea. The rise of the vast Mongol Empire allowed for safer travel conditions, and trading along the Silk Road once again prospered. In 1271 Marco Polo, the seventeen-year-old son of a Venetian merchant, traveled to the great Kublai Khan's court, where he served the Khan for many years.

Returning to the West, Marco Polo was imprisoned in Genoa. Luckily for us, he dictated his travels to a romance-writing cell mate. Published about 1305, this recounting gave an enticing description of Cathay, as China was named in medieval times. Dawn Jacobson, in her book *Chinoiserie,* says: "His [Marco Polo's] book enshrined and distilled the fabulous vision of the East held by generations of Europeans and played a starring role in the creation of Chinoiserie, a style whose very being depended on an imperfect and romantic understanding of China."

OPPOSITE

This chinoiserie design *Bamboo Grove* in the Brunschwig spring 2004 collection was based on a Chinese wallpaper found at the Château de Grancey, near Dijon, in France. The design—which bears a relationship to the Chinese wallpapers at Westbury House—has been adapted into fabric as well as wallpaper. It comes in several colorways but is shown here in a gorgeous combination of blue and tea-paper silver, perfect for a glittering powder room or a small but impressive elevator hall—or even lining the elevator itself.

ABOVE

Antique, hand-painted Chinese wallpaper in the Chippendale Guest Room at Westbury House shows a bamboo forest with birds and insects.

OPPOSITE

The Blue Guest Room in Westbury House, Old Westbury, Long Island, New York, is one of two rooms with rare, early-eighteenth-century, hand-painted Chinese wallpaper. This design with no repeats shows trees with gnarled trunks bearing flowers and foliage with whimsical birds—a Chinese interpretation of the Indian tree of life.

This romantic view was reinforced by others. Friar Odoric, a Franciscan missionary, wrote an account of three years he spent in Peking—including tales of Chinese women with bound feet, long-fingernailed mandarins, and cormorants trained to fish. *Sir John Mandeville's Travels,* a bestseller published about 1350, was translated into ten languages, and became the main source of information about China—even though the travels and author were totally fictitious.

It was not until 1669 that a book of engraved illustrations of the fabled country was published. These were by a Dutch artist, John Nieuhoff, steward to the Dutch ambassador to China. He drew the people he saw, such as priests and monks, with wonderful headdresses made of feathers and a pagoda in Nanking with a pineapple at the very top. Nieuhoff's drawings in the seventeenth and eighteenth centuries were almost as popular as magazines and newspapers are today. His illustrations even influenced the look of Western architecture—his pagoda image obviously inspired English architect Sir William Chambers, who designed the famous pagoda at Kew Gardens, in 1756. Fabrics, wallpaper, furniture, and porcelain all took on the charming, fanciful style the French dubbed chinoiserie, a style still in favor today.

When Murray Douglas was working with Westbury House on Long Island, New York, to develop rose-patterned fabrics, she went on a tour of the house. There she found two bedrooms with exemplary early Chinese wallpapers hand painted by artists. Such papers, while rare even in English houses, are very unusual in America. Many were originally presented as gifts by the great hongs, or merchant companies, to their valued customers after a major deal had been transacted. Up to the mid eighteenth century, birds and flowers were favorite motifs; after that came landscapes with figures. "Jay" Phipps, who built Westbury House for his family, was so fond of them he wanted more rooms with hand-painted Chinese wallpaper, but his English decorator, George Crawley,

dissuaded him by saying that he would be unable to hang pictures on the walls. These were artworks in themselves, with no repeats—it would be like hanging a picture on a scenic wallpaper.

When Brunschwig adapts a documentary wallpaper such as the one found at the Château de Grancey, in France, birds are usually omitted because they sometimes look a little awkward when rendered into repeats—unlike on scenic wallpapers, where no repeats occur, and the birds therefore appear more natural. However, birds are included when a design is made into fabric.

Chinoiserie seeped into all aspects of design. Chinese export porcelain filled the trading ships, along with carved-and-painted Coromandel screens (which were made in China but shipped from the Indian coast). The silk weavers of Lyon were inspired by chinoiserie designs, the earliest appearing during the reign of Louis XIV. A favorite is *Le Lac,* designed by Philippe de Lasalle as a brocaded silk. The fabric was narrow, handwoven, and lightweight because the brocading process was clipped when the weft returned to the back of the design—but it had a huge repeat. In the twentieth century, *Le Lac* was reproduced as a print using stencils on wider goods.

Aristocratic Europeans became besotted with chinoiserie when the fanciful style came to full fruition blending perfectly with the age of rococo. The modish painter François Boucher was much taken with it, painting *The Fishing Party* and *La Dolce Chinoise.* Murray Douglas points out that if they didn't have Chinese faces, they would look like Parisians

The bed hangings and bed cover in this downstairs bedroom at George Washington's house, Mount Vernon, in Virginia, are of newly installed *Chinoiserie à l'Américaine,* a design based on a Mount Vernon document. (The chinoiserie toile was also used in a golf club in Scotland decorated by Donna Vallone when she was at Wiseman & Gale; see p. 137.)

having a good time. The Palace of Drottingholm, outside Stockholm, has a pavilion, Kina, that was given to Louisa Ulrica, sister of Frederick the Great, for her thirty-fifth birthday, in 1753. It burned down and was rebuilt in brick by her husband. The entrance hall leads to a lacquer-paneled yellow room with decorations over the doors by Boucher. A blue salon inspired by the artist is highlighted in gilt. The Hunkammer, the dog room, has kennels decorated in lighthearted Pillement-style chinoiserie.

More examples following the trend include a chinoiserie *cabinet* in Copenhagen; an indoor swimming pool lined with Chinese tiles at Badenburg, near Munich, and upstairs a changing room with Chinese wallpaper and

China Fancy was a chinoiserie documentary wallpaper design found at the Winterthur Estate which was made specially for the historic house Gunston Hall. They wanted a chinoiserie-style English wallpaper for a room in this house that has wonderful chinoiserie architecture. *China Fancy* took seven years of work to get approval by the Board of Directors at Gunston Hall, This new interpretation is called *New China Fancy*. This room has had several metamorphoses; it was a dining room at one time but is now a parlor.

A New Book of CHINESE ORNAMENTS Invented & Engraved by Pillement

lacquerware and a silver-and-jonquil-yellow bedroom; a breathtaking circular room all silver and blue rococo at Amelienburg; a pagoda at Amboise (*everyone* wanted a pagoda in their gardens— perfect for garden parties), and Russian palaces around St. Petersburg with chinoiserie. Jean-Baptiste Pillement drew exquisite incorporeal pagodas that

look as if a puff of wind would blow them away. Brunschwig & Fils is so enamored of chinoiserie the company has a design called *Chinoiserie* and another called *Pillement.*

The factory at Jouy naturally included chinoiserie designs among their printed toiles. About 1760 Oberkampf presented a chinoiserie as one of his first patterns. It was indigo blue, printed with a woodblock, and showed a pagoda and a Chinese man pushing a little cart. Using the monotone toile format, Jean-Baptiste Huet used themes such as little bridges, pagodas and fretted pavilions with pointed roofs, trees with knobby trunks, outsize flowers, rock formations, bird cages, water scenes with Chinese junks, cormorants fishing, and men smoking hookahs.

In England, Chippendale—never one to miss a trend— had his workshops turn out elaborately carved and fretted-back "Chinese" chairs; an example of antique English crewelwork now at Williamsburg was inspired by chinoiserie. An English 1760 wallpaper inspired by the thought of Cathay includes a camel, a greyhound, and fantastic flowers. The Brunschwig design called *Rêve de Papillon* came from an English morning room. English artists were trained to "paint in the Chinese way."

OPPOSITE

Jean-Baptiste Pillement peopled his finely drawn mythical Chinese landscapes with robed figures and fragile pagodas.

ABOVE

The original document for the longtime favorite *Le Lac* was originally a silk brocaded with silk and chenille yarns, which gave a velvety effect, made in the eighteenth century at the height of the chinoiserie craze. Now translated into a printed fabric, it still retains its gigantic scale—and is even more popular—and is considerably less expensive.

LEFT

Julie Stander of Houston, Texas, designed this guest bathroom and commode using *New China Fancy* in a jade coloring for a house in Baton Rouge.

BELOW

Detroit designer Dan Clancy and Mark Manardo of Perlmutter-Friewald decorated this morning room for the 1998 Junior League of Detroit Designers' Showhouse. The 1910 house had Chinese wallpaper, which prompted them to choose *Empress of China* as the main print for their room. Seen here as pillows on the sofa, and also upholstering furniture, the fabric design was adapted from a set of eighteenth-century window hangings at the Winterthur Estate which had been hand painted on silk by Chinese artists aiming at the European market. *Chatillon* cut velvet covers the chair.

(They were not, as some have suggested, Chinese slaves brought to England to paint.) At Brunschwig the artists have been trained to do the same.

The Royal Pavilion at Brighton first sparked Murray Douglas's interest in chinoiserie. The over-the-top seaside palace was built about 1830 for George IV, who had for so long been the flamboyant prince regent, and the building was a homage to many exotic styles. Murray noted many details—a lantern on a pole held by a dragon, a corridor of Chinese hand paintings, an extraordinary pink and blue combination, wonderful monumental jars, a staircase of metalwork painted to resemble bamboo, and all kinds of faux paintings—images that were then incorporated into a Brunschwig collection. People have been excited about the lure of the East for a long time, and it is still appropriate for today— fanciful, cheerful, fun, uplifting.

This photograph of the entrance to the New York Brunschwig & Fils showroom shows the pale, watery colors of *Kanchou* chintz, which was upholstered to the walls in the classic way and held in place with a self piping. (*Kanchou* is also used on the walls of John Banks's bedroom vignette on p. 187.)

Manhattan antiques and
decorative accessories
store owners William Meyer
and Wayne Adler of
William/Wayne have a
glowing fantasy living
room lined with red-on-red
Cathay toile wallpaper with
the same design used for
upholstery. *Cathay* toile
was a SPNEA block-printed
document. (Also see
Cathay in blue as fabric
upholstered on Robert
Raymond's wall on p. 22
and used in Auckland,
New Zealand, on p. 133.)
The room shown here is
constantly changing and,
though crowded, proves
to be an enticing space
for evening parties.

4

Documentary Designs
Museums and
Historic Houses

The Brunschwig mystique includes a remarkable and successful relationship with superb museums and historic houses. Historic documentary designs have been a mainstay of Brunschwig & Fils. They not only contribute to beautiful, well-proportioned patterns but also provide an intellectual edge to each collection. The history behind a documentary fabric adds to its romance for both decorators and their clients.

OPPOSITE

Bicoastal designers Marie Johnston and Susan Federman at Johnston Associates, San Francisco, put together this stylish living room/game room using a longtime favorite *Rose D'Aubier* cotton-and-linen print on chairs at a game table. This design was based on a seventeenth- or eighteenth-century English crewel wool embroidery. The coloring blends unexpectedly well with the modern *Angelica Tapestry* used on the sofa pillow, producing an unusual but satisfying juxtaposition of design eras and proportions.

RIGHT

In her own dining room, Barbara Southerland of Greenville, South Carolina, used the imperial cotton print *Napoleon Trois* for curtains, emphasizing the colorway by having plenty of red on the tabletop.

In this colorful living room designed by Cody & Wolff of Jamesville, New York, the upholstery is done in a multicolor print on a white ground called *New Athos.* The fabric was developed from an eighteenth-century painted Chinese taffeta document that came from a French supplier—it was later discovered that the Winterthur Estate Museum owns a piece of the same silk. (See Ray Clarke's Ohio dining room on p. 81 for another version of the print.) The room shows international influences—a Japanese screen, an American eagle, a Brunschwig & Fils *Portuguese* coffee table— and an appropriate use of printed fabric on furniture.

The Palace of Versailles

It would be difficult to envision a grander room than the bedroom of Madame de Pompadour at Versailles. Restored and opened to the public in 2002, the room shows the height of mid-eighteenth-century French elegance, reflecting de Pompadour's sophisticated taste and personal promotion of all the decorative arts, especially French textiles and Sevres porcelain. The French had brought the production of luxe fabrics to a fine art. Weaving was patronized by royalty and later subsidized by the French government. Some of the looms that produced these exquisite complex weaves still exist. On a visit to Lyon, Murray Douglas observed many young people working there, getting master apprentice degrees in traditional weaving.

As Murray points out, fabrics and their surroundings can compel a wide range of emotion, from the conceit of delicious opulence to the serene simplicity of quiet understatement. A bequest of furniture from the Duchess of Windsor upon her death was the starting point for the restoration of Madame de Pompadour's apartment at the Château de Versailles.

Doing a watercolor of Madame de Pompadour's recently finished bedroom in her hidden Versailles apartment was a challenge for Murray. How to convey the elegance of the silk lampas—in her favorite blue-green color—that upholstered her bed-in-niche and the rococo chairs? Murray told herself to stop being uptight and just do a simple, quick sketch to suggest the color and a bit of the pattern and then contrast it with the skirted dressing table with lace-draped mirror. "I think I succeeded: a sneak peek at the elegant room, before Madame returned. . . ."

The exquisite and complex silk lampas mentioned above was made by the Lyon silk manufacturer Verel de Belval and is sold in the United States by Brunschwig & Fils International. The colors chosen were based on written documents by Madame de Pompadour, indicating her love for blue-green and pink fabrics.

OPPOSITE

Murray Douglas was so inspired by the stylish grandeur of Madame de Pompadour's bedroom at Versailles that she painted this watercolor of it. The fabric *Castel* silk used in the room in a favored blue-green colorway s based on an eighteenth-century French lampas, which s a heavier weave than brocading and, therefore, more sturdy for upholstery.

Walt Whitman House

In complete contrast to the opulence of the Palace of Versailles was a project involving documentary wallpaper designs for the simple, frugal house where the once-controversial American poet Walt Whitman lived out his latter years. Brunschwig's Tom Marshall, now director of North American sales, still keeps a hand in special design projects, and this was one of his favorites. "I am lucky," says Tom; "both Mr. Peardon and Mrs. Douglas are interested in historic preservation." Brunschwig & Fils is involved with the Metropolitan Historic Structures Organization that, together with the New Jersey Parks and Environmental Protection departments, hired architect Page Cowley of Cowley & Prudon Architects to restore the Whitman house. Tom was asked to come up with suitable wallpapers.

Whitman's house was in ruins. No documents existed except some old photographs of newspaper clippings published at the poet's death. "Not much to go on!" says Tom Marshall; "but they represented the period." Using these black-and-white clippings, he searched the Brunschwig Archive for colored documents of the period. To work out the appropriate scale and calculate the correct dimensions, he used existing architectural elements in the house, such as the fireplace surround and its relationship to the wallpapers in the photographs.

Four different wallpapers were produced for the Walt Whitman house, their names suggested by members of the New Jersey Parks and Forestry staff, based on titles of Whitman poems: *Halcyon Days* in the front parlor, *Leaves of Grass* border (which was probably *not* designed to coordinate with *Halcyon Days*), *Drum Taps* sidewall in his bedroom, and a fourth paper called *Camerado*. None has been included in the regular Brunschwig collection because the designs do not generally reflect today's taste. Whitman was not interested in modishness; his housekeeper probably simply went out and bought the paper off the shelf at the nearest shop.

OPPOSITE TOP
The restored front parlor at the Walt Whitman house.

OPPOSITE BOTTOM LEFT
A sidewall paper, *Halcyon Days,* named after a Walt Whitman poem, was reproduced as closely as possible from newspaper clippings.

OPPOSITE BOTTOM RIGHT
In Walt Whitman's restored bedroom the striped wallpaper was named *Drum Taps,* also after one of his poems.

Winterthur, An American Country Estate

Brunschwig's relationship with the H. F. DuPont Winterthur Museum (now known as Winterthur, An American Country Estate) began in the 1960s. Mrs. Brunschwig was looking for an entrée and found it through a colleague, Donald McMillen, a display adviser to Mr. DuPont. He was asked to create an introductory panel for the museum's new South Wing. Brunschwig was given the task of reproducing a Winterthur-owned, 1775, American, block-printed textile for display on vinyl (so as not to be confused with the original textile). The successful display exercise led to much discussion about a strategy for the future. In 1971 Winterthur decided to investigate creating a collection of furnishing textiles and other objects inspired by their holdings to be marketed in their retail shop. Brunschwig was asked to reproduce several designs for this purpose. Two of these, *Marlboro* and *Hampton Resist* continue to be part of the Brunschwig collection, which currently contains twenty-three fabrics and five wallpapers—all faithfully reproduced from Winthertur's wonderful archive, and we look forward to future additions to the group.

One of the documentary designs found at Winterthur, *Sun, Moon, and Stars,* is a European design of about 1790 to 1820 that has proved itself to be extremely versatile. (See pp. 146–149 for an example of how it has been brilliantly effective in a contemporary school.) Designer Leslie Christiansen used it in a unpretentious but traditional way in what is now the living room in an 1825 Brooklyn Heights farmhouse in the Federal style. The room originally would have been a basement kitchen with the formal reception rooms on the floor above, reached by a stoop. The house is the middle one of three that were part of the Pierrepont Estate. Though the whole area is now busy streets and closely packed houses, their fields then extended all the way to the water. Brooklyn Heights was considered New York's first suburb. When these houses were built, the Fulton Ferry could make it to Manhattan in five minutes. The house owners are collectors of antiques from Brooklyn and eastern Long Island, especially distinctive Dominy furniture made in East Hampton, a shop that existed for generations until it closed, after World War I.

ABOVE

Interior designer Leslie Christiansen chose a favorite documentary design found at the Winterthur Estate—*Sun, Moon, and Stars*—to decorate this basement family room (originally a kitchen) in Brooklyn Heights, New York. With the documentary print, he combined *Chloe*—a red woven texture—and *Boizot* check in yellow-orange-gold.

LEFT

In this corner of the living room, a painting—bought at Christie's—hangs above the table. Around it are fancy painted chairs in the Federal style. Other antiques include jars made in Brooklyn, an 1840 American dish, and an English pewter vessel used as a vase.

Clifton House

Chairman Tom Peardon and Vice Chairman Murray Douglas are both descendants of the Thompson family, gentry who lived in historic Clifton House, which is surrounded by the rolling landscape of Clifton Park in Baltimore. The area deteriorated from its original grandeur in the mid twentieth century but is gradually being brought back to life under an organization called Civic Works, and the imposing house is now used for education and civic events.

The dining room has been refurbished using Brunschwig fabrics and wallpaper, plus hours of dedicated work from curator Diane Wheaton, who made the handsome *Gerfalco* moiré swagged curtains and *New Richmond* dimity undercurtains (she used to run a theatrical costume workshop), and from specialist carpenter Chris Wilson, who repaired the architectural woodwork. Now known as the Thompson Room, the space is the first of—one hopes—many restored rooms to come at Clifton House.

When we went to photograph the Thompson Room, we had been prewarned that it would be dark inside because the windows were permanently boarded up for security. Realizing it would make a dreary picture without daylight, photographer Alex McLean, together with Chris Wilson, got to work removing the boards to let the sunshine in. Outside, glimpsed through the doorway, was a lovely wide porch—though this had not been in place at the time the Thompsons lived there. Baltimore decorator Stiles Colwell came up with correct garnitures for the table and mantel, Diane Wheaton picked flowers from near her own house, and another Thompson descendant, Nelson Bolton, brought pretty antique figurines to provide the finishing touch. It has since been determined that the room's long-since-lost original wallpaper had been installed specially for Henry Thompson's wedding, in 1798. This was not known at the time of the renovations. Brunschwig submitted the equally appropriate *Sheffield Arabesque* wallpaper that was finally selected.

When the Civic Works staff came to see the redesigned room, they were amazed and thrilled!

LEFT
In the Thompson Room at Clifton House, built about 1800 in Baltimore, curtains are of *Gerfalco* moiré with undercurtains of *New Richmond* dimity. The chair seats are of *Camden* woven texture. The framed portrait of Henry Thompson on the *Sheffield Arabesque* papered walls is a copy printed on canvas. Baltimore decorator Stiles Colwell and Thompson descendant Nelson Bolton lent antiques.

Historic Deerfield Collection

Historic Deerfield in Massachusetts is a museum of early New England life, consisting of fifty-two buildings, fourteen of which are carefully preserved eighteenth- and nineteenth-century houses. With its wealth of historic textile documents, it was the perfect place to inspire a Brunschwig spring 2003 collection.

Banyan, seen as bed hangings in the photograph on this page, is a printed design based on a man's dressing gown found in the Historic Deerfield Archive. These garments—also known as morning gowns or India gowns—had been worn by gentlemen in the privacy of their homes since the mid sixteenth century. Diarist Samuel Pepys wore one (he actually rented it!) when sitting for his portrait in 1666. Dressing gowns found their way to America but were worn only by the affluent. An example of a painted cotton banyan in the Historic Deerfield textile collection shows a typical design—curvilinear stripes and zigzags with peonies—from the Coromandel Coast of India, about 1775–85, when European taste was influencing Indian chintzes for export. The original design appears to have been hand stenciled and has the artist's name written on the selvedge.

Before printed fabric became commonplace, embroidery was frequently used to embellish fabric. Other designs in the Historic Deerfield collection were inspired by embroidered documents: a chintz, *Song of India,* and a cotton print, *Esther's Stitchery. Wethersfield Quilt* is a double-woven fabric, a matelassé with a quilted appearance inspired by a 1924 quilt made by Fannie Bouviere Stebbins of Wethersfield, Connecticut. She had chosen motifs for the fifty-six blocks of the handmade quilt from mid-nineteenth-century advertisements in ladies' magazines, *cartes de visite* of the period, and early photographs.

RIGHT

The village of Historic Deerfield in Massachusetts inspired a Brunschwig collection. When photographed, this four-poster bed was dressed with *Banyan* cotton print—one of the collection's fabrics. The bed was so handsome and showcased the fabric so well that it was given a place in the New York showroom. Blue-and-white *Coventry Coverlet* is on the bed, and a *Guerrero* mirror is on the wall. On the *Quebec* table by the bed is a *Trunc* lamp, and on the far side is an urn-shaped *Coalport* lamp. *Indian Spring* figured woven covers the bench at the foot of the bed.

Cabanel Collection   The Brunschwig design team visited André-Jean Cabanel, a Provençal vine and olive farmer, who had amassed a glorious collection of one thousand quilts, silks, and cottons. "When I began collecting antique quilts and textiles, people used to laugh at me," recounts Cabanel; "'what are you doing with all those old rags?' they'd say." Now his sumptuous collection, garnered over thirty years (mainly from armoires in the bourgeois houses of southern France), is considered to be the most important of its kind in the world.

Living in the hills to the west of Nîmes—the town that gave to the world the term *denim* (from *de Nîmes*)—Cabanel as a boy would watch his

OPPOSITE

One of Brunschwig's most endearing collections was based on a hoard of antique Provençal quilts accumulated by André-Jean Cabanel. Their warmhearted and colorful appeal can be clearly seen in these packed shelves. Some of the fabrics inspired by that collection include *Gardanne* figured woven, *Sommières* cotton print, *Isle sur Sorgues* figured woven, and *Cigalou* cotton print.

ABOVE

For Ross and Mac Francis, William Kulp decorated this New York bedroom en suite using *Le Kakatoès,* a toile introduced in the Cabanel collection that has become a new "classic."

RIGHT

A doorway passage at the Inn at Little Washington, a famous and a much-sought-after escape for Washington, D.C., politicos, shows *Nanou Rockery* wallpaper. The imaginative, amusing, and sometimes surprising decoration was done by English set designer Joyce Evans. (For other photographs of this inn, see pp. 138–141.)

mother as she repaired quilts. He loved the rich, bright colors that could stand up so well to the Provençal sun.

Among the selected fabrics adapted from Cabanel's cache is what has now become a new "classic" toile, *Le Kakatoès,* showing a bucolic world of harvesters, lovers, and domestic animals. *Nanou Rockery* is adapted from the stylized "ground" of a hand-stenciled, hand-painted indienne palampore from about 1793 (see the doorway passage at the Inn at Little Washington on p. 55; Thomas Hamel's use of it in Australia on p. 131; its use in the entrance to the North White Plains corporate headquarters on p. 206; and Dennis Rolland's vignette on p. 157. The original was a late-eighteenth-century, block-printed design. The details were outlined in black using a copper roller. *Isle sur Sorgues,* a figured double woven cotton made in France, has a flower stripe on one side and a tiny check on the other. It was adapted from a late-eighteenth-century striped cotton embroidered in silk thread with a simple flower motif (see Olivier and Susannah Peardon's apartment in Paris on p. 114).

Egremont A fruitful collaboration between Brunschwig and the Society for the Preservation of New England Antiquities (SPNEA) resulted in a design called *Egremont.* A hand-block design of a cow and a calf combined with a lace-and-herringbone stripe that had been used as a wallpaper in the Vogler House, one of SPNEA's properties. In the Brunschwig Archive was an 1815–25 document with a kindred design, showing a boy with a dog. It had scattered motifs and vertical stripes and a tree spreading above the boy. The two designs had such an affinity they could have been carved by the same block maker. Brunschwig's Studio married the two designs and used the result as both a cotton print

OPPOSITE TOP

An 1815–25 document found in the Society for the Preservation of New England Antiquities (SPNEA) archive was married to a Brunschwig & Fils archival document of the same period. Together the two formed the design *Egremont.* This photograph shows how it was featured on a Bob Vila television program about SPNEA. The room was decorated by designer Leslie Curtis.

OPPOSITE BOTTOM

On the advice of their architect, Dennis Wedlick, David Rockwell and Richard Weinstein used *Egremont* wallpaper in the bathroom of their house in Chatham, New York. The original two designs that were combined to form *Egremont* were created at a time when rural life was seen as romantic.

and as a wallpaper. The home-decorating
television show host Bob Vila produced a
segment about SPNEA that described its work
with museums and historic houses. He told the
story of *Egremont* and featured the fabric on
a wicker settee in a porch setting.

Westbury House   Old Westbury

Gardens on Long Island, New York, was the
country estate of the John (Jay) Shaffer Phipps
family. Jay's father, Henry, had been a partner in
Andrew Carnegie's iron-and-steel company and
was known as a great philanthropist and avid
horticulturalist. A few years ago, Murray
Douglas gave a lecture at Old Westbury
Gardens entitled "Fabrics in Bloom." Her topic
could not have been more suited to the
surroundings. Completed in 1907, Westbury
House is encircled by glorious gardens that
change with the seasons. Brunschwig & Fils
found two floral chintzes that they named after
the house—*Westbury Roses,* which on a white
ground is used in the White Drawing Room
seen on pp. 58–59, and *Westbury Bouquet,*
with its rich, aubergine background. Both
were developed from hand-blocked English
designs of plump, overblown flowers. These
designs demonstrate how the West developed
realistic-looking flowers compared to the
purely fantastic flowers of Indian printed
chintz. (See *Westbury Bouquet* used on the
overscaled sofas of the West Porch on p. 95.)

OVERLEAF

The White Drawing Room at Westbury House,
Long Island, New York, with its comfortable,
overstuffed furniture covered in *Westbury Roses,*
is where members of the Phipps family would
gather to have afternoon tea. The design was
developed from a nineteenth-century English
hand-blocked chintz, with the repeat made
slightly smaller to accommodate today's scale
of furniture.

Mount Vernon

One of the most long-lasting liaisons between Brunschwig and a historic house has been with George Washington's home, Mount Vernon, in Virginia. It is also one of Murray Douglas's favorite houses. Over the years many Brunschwig fabrics have been developed and used there. As related in *Brunschwig & Fils Style,* the "Lafayette" bedroom was originally restored with a toile appropriate for the period. A letter from the French statesman Lafayette to his family was subsequently discovered. In it, he describes the room as decorated with an indienne design. The bedroom was then redone in French indienne *Creil.* In April 2003, a new colorway of *Creil* replaced the old one. The new coloring was made from a recently found document that had not been exposed to light, so it had retained its original vivid coloring. Now the bed hangings are as Lafayette would have seen them when he slept there. In the letter to his family, he mentioned that he loved the Mount Vernon bedroom. In the late eighteenth century, people yearned for printed fabric to have true white grounds rather than the more easily obtained cream or natural ones. To achieve the desired white required time-consuming bleaching in the sun each time a new dye was added.

This brings up the importance of paint colors in a room, which are as much a part of the general look of any space as the fabrics used. In a bedroom at Mount Vernon, paint expert

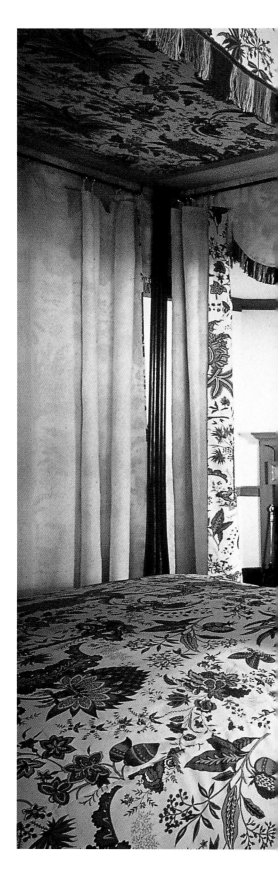

Matthew Mosca scraped back twenty-six layers of paint to the original coat, which was a very bright blue-green—quite garish to our eyes. The muted Old Williamsburg colors had been used as a standard for a historic look and had been implanted in American minds in the twentieth century for so long that people were shocked when these newly researched bright colors appeared. Murray Douglas has a theory that the early colonists knew certain colors were fugitive, so they made them purposely bright, expecting them to fade. Today's chemically made paints do not fade to the same extent. Mount Vernon has adopted wired lights that look just like real candle flames, which add greatly to the atmosphere.

Other recent developments with Mount Vernon include bed hangings of that unassuming American fabric *New Richmond* dimity for the Washington bedchamber seen here. We waited to see the photograph—taken just before we handed in our text to the publisher—of George Washington's newly redone bedroom at Mount Vernon, which is in the simplest cotton dimity with a self stripe. The dimity was rewoven to replace the hangings, which had become limp and yellow with age. We knew it would be breathtaking, and it was heartwarming in its white purity and total unpretentiousness. Ah, the lure of fabric. . . .

OPPOSITE

At Mount Vernon the mahogany bedstead in the Washington bedchamber that Martha Washington had "caused to be made in Philadelphia" has been newly dressed in early 2004 with *New Richmond* dimity. Bed hangings, bedding, curtains, and slipcovers have all been hand sewn from dimity, which is a light cotton material with a subtle rib. Dimity became extremely fashionable as a furnishing textile during the last decade of the eighteenth century, so it is no surprise that George and Martha Washington selected it for their own chamber.

The mahogany bed in this room was willed to Martha Washington's grandson, who indicated the bed was draped with "white dimity curtains." Window hangings, bedding, and slipcovers are all of dimity, which is in keeping with George Washington's documented preference that the furnishing textiles in a room match. Dimity is unpretentious and American in its simplicity. Its use here shows that it can be elegant, though it is not usually formal enough for most Europeans of importance.

Another Mount Vernon bedroom with new hangings of the toile de Jouy *Chinoiserie à l'Américaine* can be seen on p. 32.

The White House

It is a big leap from the home of America's first president to the White House, the place where all our presidents live while in office. One of Tom Marshall's special projects was to develop a wallpaper for the Blue Room and a table for the Cross Hall and later, during the George W. Bush administration, to suggest fabric for the Oval Office curtains.

In 1990, the Committee for the Preservation of the White House—which included then curator Betty Monkton; Kaki Hockersmith, decorator to the Clintons; the late Mark Hampton; Richard Nylander, a great authority and author on wallpapers; Tom Savage of Sotheby's; and other decorative arts historians—recommended that the Blue Room be redone in keeping with the style found in America during the first quarter of the nineteenth century. In essence, the committee wanted to step away from the more decidedly French style that was installed in the Blue Room in 1972. The refurbishment—estimated at $358,000—was paid for by the White House Endowment Fund, which raised money from private donors.

Part of the refurbishment included installation of a new reproduction wallpaper. The sidewall, the document of which comes from SPNEA, is American and dates to around 1820. The ceiling and dado borders, both reproduced from documents at the Cooper-Hewitt Museum, are French from around 1815 and echo the flavor of the 1817 French Empire chairs, chosen by President James Monroe.

Then–First Lady Hillary Rodham Clinton adopted a very hands-on approach to the project, reviewing

BELOW
This French Empire damask was the original document in the Brunschwig Archive used to develop three adaptation patterns.

RIGHT
Two red-on-red adaptation damasks developed from the Empire document made especially for the Clinton White House were used for upholstery (as seen) and curtains for the stair hall (not seen).

artwork, colors, and strike-offs. When the swag ceiling border was to be installed, it was Mrs. Clinton who noticed it didn't look quite "right," and it was she who suggested cutting out part of a brown shadow, and letting the sidewall paper peek through. The effect was subtle, but it enhanced the overall trompe l'oeil flavor of the border.

For curtains and upholstery in the Cross Hall, Brunschwig found in its Archive a dilapidated French Empire damask document, a remnant of it seen on p. 64. According to a great tome about French fabrics—*Paris, Mobilier National, series Empire*—the damask was originally made for the throne room at the Tuileries. It has a Napoleonic flavor with its wreaths and stars which worked perfectly in the White House. This fabric was woven exclusively for the Clinton White House.

For curtains behind the desk in the Oval Office during the George W. Bush administration, Brunschwig's *Raphael* damask in a bronze colorway was selected. The designer chose it because it was "regal, rich, and royal."

Brunschwig archivist Judy Straeten maintained documents, strike-offs, and slides of the artwork for the Brunschwig Archive, documenting the project from beginning to end.

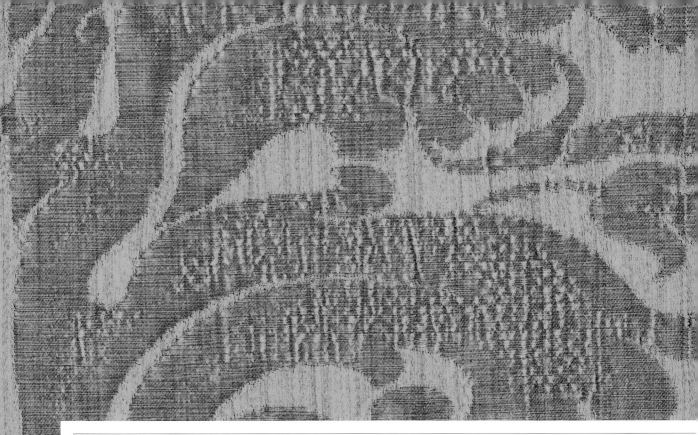

The Oval Office at the George W. Bush White House was decorated with curtains made by Brunschwig & Fils in bronze-colored *Raphael* damask.

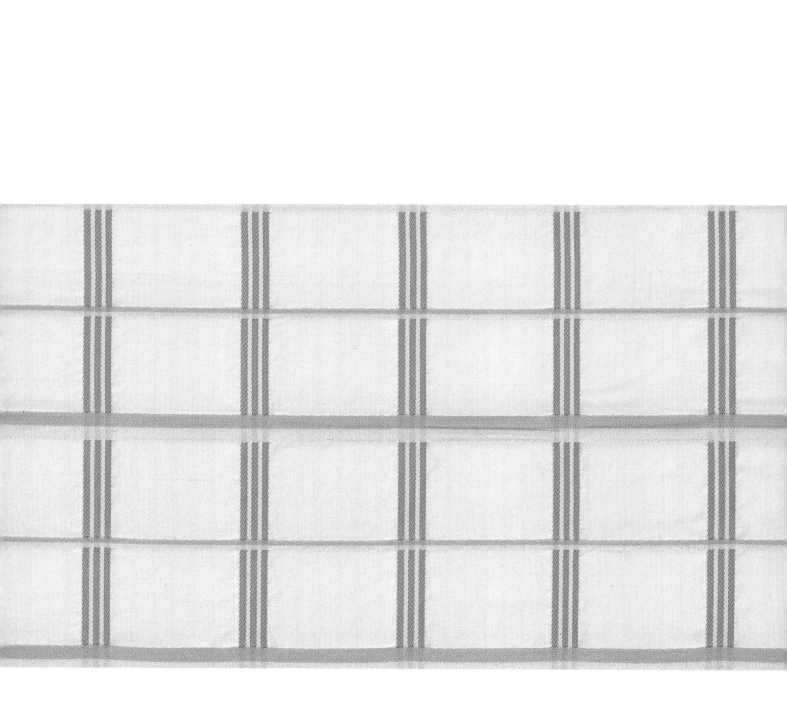

Part Two
How We Live Today

5

The State of Decoration
Private Spaces

The patterns of our lives are always changing, and with them, the use of our rooms. Here is a sampling of designers' work that reflects the way we live today and perhaps tomorrow.

Murray Douglas first met architect/designers Bernt Heiberg and William Cummings in Norway, where they had lived, but they have since moved to New York. They showed her a scheme with sketches using Brunschwig fabrics which they were planning for a weekend house in the Hamptons, Long Island, New York. Murray was intrigued by the plan's ingenuity and seeming simplicity. A strong Nordic sensibility came through in its unpretentious choice of material and lack of clutter. The house was planned in beige and natural tones but with differing textures. The floors were concrete and the walls white, and the design was full of inventive ideas for living. Shelves had an industrial flavor, being hung on poles attached to the ceiling. Plain curtains were hung the same way. The house is now finished and exudes an unexpected warmth. Though William Cummings has been quoted as saying the fabric is "French linen and American burlap," he and his partner collect textiles and know that because the open-plan spaces are so unadorned, it is essential that the monotone fabrics be of the best quality. All are nuanced, darkened naturals with a cosmopolitan pedigree. Curtains are *Ninon Taffetas* silk with a *Liso Cadiz* wool lining, but the muted sludge color belies the precious quality. One bedroom has a headboard and blankets of *Franela* wool and nylon, *Astorga* viscose and cotton from Spain,

PREVIOUS SPREAD
Luna silk plaid is made of 100 percent silk from China. It has a taffeta weave ground with a satin over plaid.

OPPOSITE
This up-close photograph of a contemporary living room by Australian designer Lill Reid uses beige *Impala* from the Gaston y Daniela collection (see p. 211 for more about the collection) on the sofa and a *Copa* lacquered lamp made in Vietnam has the serene mood that we need to counteract our stressful lives.

71

LEFT

New York architect/designers Bernt Heiberg and William Cummings of Heiberg Cummings Design Ltd. designed this exemplary modern house in the Hamptons for themselves, using fabric sparsely but in perfect accord with the tone of the spaces.

ABOVE

In the kitchen area of the Heiberg-Cummings house, all the fabrics, including simple blinds, are of the best Brunschwig materials, whether natural fibers or synthetic blends. Great ideas abound especially in the kitchen, where implements and room dividers hang from ceiling poles.

combined with *Fontaine* hand embroidery on linen from India. Blanket pillows are of *Nashville* woven texture and *Sunshine* silk in a color called twilight.

The furniture ranges from distressed painted furniture to the odd eighteenth-century chair, blended with some ingenious pieces from their *hcd3* collection. It is a fine example of a truly modern house that delights the eye.

In many contemporary houses and apartments, the living room has developed several different functions—and continues to develop more. Sometimes it is a casual family room, perhaps equipped with plasma televisions, a bar, and complex music and media gadgets. Some living rooms and drawing rooms have a formal function and are used mainly for social gatherings and receptions—afternoon tea, conversation, cocktails before dinner, coffee afterward—a less-straitlaced version of the Victorian parlor.

Many people still yearn for large and impressive living rooms—"great rooms." These require extra-large, overscaled, overstuffed, comfortable-looking furniture.

In many houses, and even more often in apartments, living rooms and dining rooms are combined in an open plan so that one can move effortlessly from the comfortable upholstered sofas and armchairs of the sitting area to the dining area, which is usually located near the kitchen for easy serving.

Grand formal dinners, with starched linen, sparkling glasses, and polished silver in a splendid setting are becoming rarer because of our casual lives. Families often eat right in the kitchen. But when the formal dining room is used, the food and ambience seem more luxurious, more "designed." Often, unless the owner has frequent dinner parties, the formal dining room is used for family gatherings in the holidays but in between may even be taken over as a home office.

With the increased use of the computer and Internet, the home office has become important. The decoration of this functional room has not generally been resolved into a pleasing aesthetic formula because so much of the necessary equipment is bland and always looks—and is—temporary. The challenge of making office space attractive is being met by designers in various ways; see, for example, Virginia Smith's office for an executive on pp. 150–151,

This library and landing in an unconventionally decorated but exuberant New Jersey household (with eight children!) was designed by New York architect/designers Carl D'Aquino and Francine Monaco for clients who, they said, "had a tremendous affection for eighteenth-century furniture and the entire blue spectrum." The fabric seen here on chair, sofa, and ottoman is *Volterra* in off-white and Genoa blue. (See p. 17 for a close-up of another room in the house.)

This 2001 Atlanta Symphony Showhouse family room is the kind of "great room" that requires large-scale furnishings. Designer Joy McLean covered the eighty-four-inch *Howard* looseback sofa and *Vincent* chairs with sable-colored *Constable* flannel. In front of the fire is a *Patrick* ottoman upholstered in moss *Zambezi gros point*. The wall covering is *Shagreen* in jasper color. The throw on the sofa is of *Bietry* woven paisley. The curtains are *Aubusson* printed tapestry.

BELOW

This Palm Beach house, originally built by Maurice Fatio, shows the master architect's touches in the tiled stairs in the family room, which is divided by a counter from the kitchen. Keith Irvine of Irvine & Fleming used blue-and-white *Villandry* linen as the theme print, with *Kelibia* woven texture in *azul royale.*

RIGHT

Oakland decorator Kay Dunne designed this living/dining room space in Burlingame, California, using *Villandry* printed linen in a bright, multicolored combination. (*Villandry* can be seen used in blue and white on this page in the breakfast room in Palm Beach.)

Nan Heminway's office for Murray Douglas on p. 180, and Robert Raymond's toile-lined office on p. 22.

Our bedrooms are a final retreat. There, we simply please ourselves. We can choose Spartan simplicity, a riot of glamorous silk, a cozy chintz, a froth of lace. Husbands traditionally—and many still today—prefer to think of the bedroom as the wife's domain . . . and it is the one place where they cherish the ultrafeminine ambience.

In a more contemporary vein, Boston designer Michael Carter created a handsome classic bedroom in neutral tones with subtle stripes, and the rug as its only obvious pattern. His black four-poster bed gives the needed "black line" that English architect Sir Edwin Lutyens insisted "every room should have," way back at the beginning of the twentieth century. At the beginning of the twenty-first century, "a black line" shows up continually—in hard-frame furniture, wallpaper outlines, black lacquer touches, and picture frames, giving much-needed punch to naturally toned rooms.

OPPOSITE TOP

Inspired by blue-and-white porcelain, Ray Clarke of Miller-Clarke Interiors in Cleveland, Ohio, decorated this vast, low-ceilinged living/dining room. He provided two tables with seats and still left room for a dance or party and played the blue-and-white *Athos* cotton print against the white walls and white floor tiles.

OPPOSITE BOTTOM

Ray Clarke decorated this bed-sitting room using the print *Anemones* to feature a collection of Japanese prints formerly owned by architect Frank Lloyd Wright.

OVERLEAF

In Vero Beach, Florida, Susan Schuyler Smith, of Spectrum, designed a straightforward living room that is both traditional and modern for a family with two young daughters. With no curtains, a pale yellow background, and a sisal rug setting the scene, the blue-and-white *La Granadina* cotton-and-linen print on sofas and armchairs delights the eye as a bold pattern. The dark finish on the furniture insinuates a Caribbean Colonial style, and the easygoing materials suggest a vacation home. The ottoman is upholstered in blue-and-white *Zambezi gros point*.

In Australia, Melbourne designer Lill Reid decorated this family room. Despite no important architecture or any curtains, it has a peaceful contemporary style, with a glass screen door, shelves with ceramics, a chimney breast flanked with books, and a burning fire. The fabric she chose is *Sonia* figured plaid in red and gold.

Patrick Gallagher of Decorative and Design in Stonington, Connecticut, designed this sitting room for the home of an American antique collector from Providence, Rhode Island. Against the *Islington* wallpaper hang well-chosen paintings. *Nangis* stripe is used on the settee. In contrast to the other rooms in this section, this is unabashedly a collector's room with a traditional but comfortable, erudite, and personal sensibility.

This room setting showcases
the Brunschwig & Fils spring
2004 collection and uses a
series of neutral colors with
sharp accents and outlines in
black—an observable trend
in contemporary decoration.

ABOVE

Christian Huebner of San Mateo, California, designed this relaxed-looking bedroom with a duvet-covered bed. For color and pattern, he used muted plaid silk *Phoebe Ann,* employing it for the back pillow, dust ruffles, curtains, and matching blind. Trimming the curtain and blind is *Applause* fringe. The wallpaper is *Chartwell* jaspé. *Morgan* lamps are on either side of the bed.

RIGHT

Boston designer Michael Carter decorated this gentleman's bedroom retreat for the 2000 Junior League Showhouse. He used geometric woven fabrics, *Lord Byron* stripe from the Italian Decortex collection, *Luna* silk plaid (pp. 68–69), and *Chartwell* jaspé stripe in a modern way, yet the effect is timeless and calm with a nonaggressive masculine feel.

6

Romantic Places
Porches, Rustic Hideaways, and Second Homes

One of Murray Douglas's favorite lectures is "Cottages Ornés," in which she discusses and shows slides of wonderful examples of rustic rooms. Some of you will remember a Brunschwig & Fils collection Cottage Orné, which featured a fanciful "Gothick" cottage in Ireland and fabrics by the Irish designer Sybil Connelly (many of them still popular today). We have extended this pastoral idyll idea to show everything from porches, follies, gazebos, and pergolas to romantic bedrooms, bathrooms, mountain ski lodges, and far-off hideaways. In her lecture Murray includes such grand places as *Le Hameau,* Marie Antoinette's fantasy hamlet and farm, where she dressed as a milkmaid and pretended to live in a "simple," bucolic way—at ruinous expense! This "return to nature" was fanned by the writings of Jean-Jacques Rousseau and other philosophes of the eighteenth-century French Enlightenment. Painter Jean-Antoine Watteau, in his *Embarkation for Cythera* (1717–19), depicted French aristocrats in silks and satins heading off to a sylvan island of love at which they will never arrive. In the twentieth century, director Federico Fellini showed extravagantly dressed members of Roman society venturing into picturesque ruins in the movie *La Dolce Vita* (1960).

Today's city folk often have a romantic vision of the countryside and long to get away to somewhere peaceful for a

91

ABOVE

This rustic pergola in Chatham, New York (called The Firefly Theater) is where Murray and Albert Douglas sit on summer evenings and watch the fireflies dance. The seat pads are covered in *La Seyne* check.

RIGHT

Movies from the 1940s on show us romantic rooms in lodges with open stone fireplaces and casual furniture for lounging. Here, in Hunting Valley, Ohio, Carol Lynn Forman designed a contemporary version. She used *Planter's Plaid* on a pair of *Howard* looseback chairs and ottoman and *Forêt de Compiegne* on the *Howard* sofa.

rustic picnic, not necessarily grand, but less formal than city life and closer to nature. For those interested in gardening, a potting room might serve this purpose, as might a porch with plants or a modest pergola with a comfortable place to read. The bedroom might have a window with a fantastic view of craggy peaks, or a sleeping porch by the beach could be just the place. The getaway home should be once removed from ordinary life, whether it is an overscaled lodge room with a huge rugged stone fireplace or a tiny, snug cabin in the mountains.

With imagination, bedrooms can transport a being on land as readily as a ship at sea, as the French surrealist poet Alfred Jarry wrote—an inspiration for Maxime de la Falaise, who felt her bed was *"un bateau qui ne navigue que sur terre, et dont les voiles sont d'antiques teintures brodées afghanes"* (a boat that moves only on land and whose sails are made of ancient Afghan embroidered hangings).

LEFT

What better for a child with a romantic imagination than this glorious playroom with a stage upon which to act out fantasies. Designed by North Carolina decorator Virginia Zenke, of The Zenkes Inc., the raised stage covers storage drawers. The stage area is wallpapered in *Forêt Foliage* (see p. 122 for the same design in autumnal coloring and p. 98 for a rusticated bathroom in the same green colorway). The curtains are of *Essex* woven plaid, which has more of an ikat effect than a simple gingham. The watercolor is by Murray Douglas.

ABOVE

One of the most successful and popular spaces at Westbury House at Old Westbury Gardens on Long Island, New York, is the screened-in West Porch. In the winter it is glassed in with hydraulically lifted windows. This porch was part of a 1924 extension, and much of its charm comes from the rough-hewn beams contrasting with the highly finished stonework. The extra-large sofas are upholstered in *Westbury Bouquet,* a design developed from a hand-blocked English chintz.

OPPOSITE

This adventurous bedroom was designed for a client by Carter Campbell, of Carter Campbell Design Group, as a guest room to be used mainly by six young nieces and nephews. The striking theme print is *Black Pepper*. *Châtillon* cut velvet in green is used on a cushion.

TOP

Decorator Nan Heminway designed this guest bedroom in Old Chatham, New York, for Murray and Albert Douglas. The theme was set by the rustic twig wallpaper *Kennebec* and by *The Walnut Tree* cotton print with its beautifully drawn birds' nests. Its touches of purplish crimson color inspired Murray to collect mulberry faience for the room.

ABOVE

New York designer Sheila Camera Kotur decorated this tranquil bedroom for a house in the Adirondacks. The drapery over the bed is *Petra* woven linen, and the cotton bedspread is *Bridgewater* matelassé.

Decorator Carter Campbell chose the exciting cotton print *Black Pepper* for a guest bedroom that would be used mainly by visiting nieces and nephews. He selected the print in order to create an interesting environment for the children while also making it sophisticated enough for grownups. The tropical African pattern proved to be fascinating for the children but not in any way juvenile. The print, which has a large repeat, "pops off" the rich, red walls. It has been used flat in its entirely so the design can be read almost like a piece of art in the room. Fourteen framed prints on the wall are from an early-nineteenth-century English book, *The World in Miniature.* The subjects seem almost to be taken directly from the fabric. With black Venetian blinds, the room spells charmed exploration and adventure.

Outside, the growing interest in gardening has spawned garden furniture, gazebos, pool houses, and fanciful follies that help give form and

OPPOSITE

This master bathroom with its dark wood cabinet and wash basin is tucked up high in the mountains. It was designed by Ginny Stine of Jacksonville, Florida, using the tapestry-effect *Forêt Foliage* wallpaper in its green combination. (See the watercolor of Virginia Zenke's children's room on p. 94 and William Stubbs's cottage in Ukraine on p. 122 for an autumn coloring.)

ABOVE

Murray Douglas's watercolor of this simple but dreamy bedroom shows Ohio designer Anne Weinberg's choice of the print *Sailors' Yarns* in blue and white. The print is based on "woollies," nautical embroideries sewn by sailors on their long sea voyages. The printed fabric has been echoed in paint on the side cupboard.

LEFT

The settee on this elegantly architectural porch is covered with *Villa Melzi* blue-and-white print, chosen by Atlanta, Georgia, designer Ginny Magher.

OPPOSITE

Ginny Magher also created this cool, dreamy Southern bedroom in a palette of cream and blue hues. The print is *Weston Park* glazed chintz, which was designed in Mulhouse about 1855 and is now printed in England. The bed valance is reflected above the eighteenth-century, limestone mantel in an antique trumeau from an old *hôtel particulier* in Aix-en-Provence.

OPPOSITE

Cleveland designer Toni Burke decorated this solarium using the large-scale print *Tea Introduction* to complement Chinese doors leading to a library. Scenes from the design have been skillfully placed on chairs. The valance, with its thirty-eight jade tassels, and the pillows on the white *Tabitha*-covered sofa are of *Couture* figured stripe. The tumbled marble floor is in a shell design to give width to the room.

RIGHT

Liz Mitchell of Marblehead, Massachusetts, designed this potting shed using the pear print *Bartlett* in "velum" (a neutral, beige hue).

whimsy to a garden. All these need a designer's touch in the choice of fabrics suitable for the outdoors. Brunschwig has developed the Outdoor Living collection with new fabrics that are lightfast, mildew resistant, pleasant to the touch, and printable.

Some porches are large and give a sense of formality, such as the Edwardian conservatories where tea might have been served by a butler and where now people gather for drinks or dinner. The grand solarium designed by Toni Burke is such a room, with its fountain, heirlooms, antiques, and comfortable furniture. It is cleverly decorated to give an impression of the grandeur that existed in Bratenhal, a Cleveland suburb, at the beginning of the twentieth century—even though the space is part of a high-rise condominium and only ten by thirty feet!

ABOVE

Chicago designer Rod Maxwell's porch for the Barrington, Ohio, Junior Women's Club Showhouse in spring 2002 used *Tanguy's Trophies* as a theme print portraying cartouches of gardening tools. Another fabric is *Eden* embroidery, which depicts flowers and butterflies sewn in shades of blue on hand-loomed cotton. Also seen in the setting are *Reggio Cassone* vases, a *Gothic* pedestal, and a *Tulip* lamp.

RIGHT

Gahanna, Ohio, designer Sandy Heifner, of Contemporary 1880, decorated this color-filled loggia with its sun-bleached pillars using red-on-Dijon *Grilly* cotton print, a French design developed from an embroidery. Cushions are covered in woven cotton *Kunming* from Spain. Also seen is *La Seyne* check, which comes from India.

Because it is a showhouse space, Rod Maxwell's fairly elaborate porch has a sense of display not usually found in porches and patios. The print *Tanguy's Trophies,* with its classical conceit of garden implements arranged into cartouches, gives it a certain historic swagger, as does *Eden* embroidery, which is sewn on hand-loomed cotton. The embroidery in tones of blue is hand guided, worked on a sewing machine (see the swatch on p. 223). All the furniture in this showhouse setting is from Brunschwig & Fils.

Porches in the Midwest need to be colorful because of the long, overcast winters and the clouds thrown off by the Great Lakes. Sandy Heifner, of Contemporary 1880, put plenty of vibrancy into the loggia seen on the facing page. She chose a daring palette of reds and golds—no neutrals for her! The

pillows, covered in a cotton called *Kunming* woven, from Spain, have been imaginatively used on the less-obvious mustard color side, though the red side is the "finished" side—a case of breaking the rules to advantage. The space is large and is divided into a dining area and a sitting area. Windows with grilles face the main house, while the loggia overlooks a garden. The effect is robust but refined.

Irishman Nicholas Mosse and his American wife, Susan, have a hand-thrown and sponge-decorated pottery business in an old family mill at Bennettsbridge, County Kilkenny, Ireland, which uses the River Noire to produce its electricity. The Mosses had been told that there once had been a rustic cottage and waterfall on their property nearby, but they did not discover them until a tremendous storm in 1996 loosened built-up silt, and the stream with its waterfall appeared. They located the foundations of the cottage and rebuilt it, complete with its thatched roof, greatly enhancing the original landscape and the appeal of their already-romantic situation. When Murray Douglas visited them, she was so taken with the idyllic scene that she painted the watercolor below.

OPPOSITE

This watercolor by Murray Douglas shows afternoon tea outside a cottage orné near Kilkenny, Ireland. The house belongs to Nicholas and Susan Mosse, who run a flourishing hand-thrown and sponge-decorated pottery business. The tablecloth is the well-known *Brunschwig Plaid* which is often seen in gray and white but here in green and white. The rustic pottery is from Nicholas Mosse, of course.

ABOVE

Rosemary Burgher of Cedar Hill, New York, designed this garden room, which "encompassed everything I love, from gardening to the earthy palette we used." She employed the print *Flew the Coop* as well as *Rayure Fleurette* stripe, *Hancock* woven plaid, *Surrey* woven texture, and *Vintage Trellis* wallpaper. Murray Douglas's watercolor of the room captures the "earth-on-her-hands" kind of space.

ROMANTIC PLACES | 107

Albert and Virginia Callan
enjoy spending winters in
Mexico so much that they
settled for a fishing shack
on a lake in the New York
Berkshires during the
summer. Brunschwig fabrics
saved the day! On the
chairs are *Tahiti* print, and
Oh Susannah stripe is on
the table. (Albert Callan
has a bathroom with
Bibliothèque which he
calls the library.) Watercolor
by Murray Douglas.

7

Home Thoughts from Abroad
Overseas Decorating

Brunschwig & Fils is enjoying a growing international market for its products. Since *Brunschwig & Fils Style* was published, in 1995, new showrooms have opened all over the world, the most recent one in Dubai, United Arab Emirates. Here is a portfolio of rooms by designers from Russia to Indonesia to New Zealand.

In France—the country that is Brunschwig & Fils' original and spiritual home—is Chairman Tom Peardon and his wife, Eveline's, house, which is small but charming, set near the town of Bayeux, in Normandy. This town is famous for the Bayeux Tapestry, which commemorates the 1066 Battle of Hastings and the Norman invasion of England. (In a book about textiles, one must add that it was not a "tapestry" at all, but was embroidered.) Eveline Peardon has created a comfortable, inviting bijou abode in which to relax from the stress of business. Being French, Eveline comes from the great tradition of perfecting the arts of peace; she not only has excellent taste with *le décor* but also is an accomplished cook, and both Peardons enjoy their pretty garden.

Their son, Olivier, and his wife, Susannah, maintain an apartment in Paris. They are a young couple starting out in married life. The apartment is unpretentious but has a European sophistication. French doors lead to a wrought-iron balcony, and the rooms have the polished wood floors and tall ceilings found in many Parisian apartments. The furnishings are simple, almost sparse, as can be expected in a starter apartment.

OPPOSITE

Tom and Eveline Peardon's living room in their house in Bayeux, France, has *Kangshi* print on the *méridienne*. The curtains and a chair are of red, blue, and white *Tartarin* woven plaid. In the foreground is a red-painted *Pennyscroll* table.

In the dining room of Tom and Eveline Peardon's house in Bayeux, France, *Luneville* panel wallpaper is a trompe l'oeil of the traditional penchant of hanging precious porcelain plates on walls. Wittily, some real ones are hung, too. The chair seats are of *Fer Doré* woven texture.

Susannah attends to the decorating and reveals here a subtle, nuanced sense of color and a great eye for personal details. She does much of the sewing herself: she made the dining room curtains from *Isle sur Sorgues,* a reversible cotton from the Cabanel collection, which has a blue-and-white flowered stripe on one side and a tiny check on the reverse. Susannah sewed a *giselle*—fan-edged trimming—on the leading edge but turned the check to the right side on the other edge and finished it as a decorative, narrow-checked hem, which is also the lining of the curtains. *Isle sur Sorgues* is "finished"—that is, trimmed and inspected—on both sides, and it is displayed in two places in showrooms, with checks and with figured textures. Susannah was busy putting together the nursery for their new baby when these photographs were taken.

ABOVE

The living room in Olivier and Susannah Peardon's Paris apartment has chair covers of white linen and a pillow of *Le Zèbre* print.

RIGHT

The slanting Parisian light catches a corner of the Peardons' bedroom. The curtains are of *Charlotte strié* faille; the Chinese-inspired wallpaper is *Kanchou* (see p. 37 for its use in the New York showroom and p. 187 for John Banks's bedroom).

ABOVE

The baby's nursery has walls and curtains of *Marianthi Flowers* (named after the Brunschwig artist Marianthi Raptis, who designed it). For a nice touch, on the changing table a round box is covered with wallpaper.

RIGHT

For curtains and chair seats in their dining room in Paris, Susannah Peardon chose *Isle sur Sorgues* figured woven (see Cabanel collection p. 54).

An amusing hallway in Belgium by Suzy Clé and Koen Van Gestel of Trendson Interieur uses a wallpaper depicting a playful monkey circus. It is called *A Tribute to John S. Churchill,* after the artist who designed it. Sally Baring, John Churchill's daughter, finds fabric and wallpaper designs for Brunschwig & Fils. (See another use of it by Audrey Morgan on p. 190.)

Copenhagen designer Anne Nexøe Larsen decorated this room in the Christian VII palace, Copenhagen, Denmark. A palace that Hans Christian Andersen visited many times between 1856 and 1875 (one of the guest rooms is named after him), it is in a typically straightforward neoclassic Danish style. Larsen used blue-and-white *Bayberry* woven texture for this room's walls and daybed.

In addition to Madame de Pompadour's apartments in the Palace of Versailles, Brunschwig fabric was used in the much simpler Christian VII palace, in Copenhagen. Denmark is known for its unpretentious, neoclassic palaces and manor houses, as well as for its porcelain and chandeliers. To quote San Francisco decorator Anthony Hail, who is of Danish extraction, "They have gilding, but not too much." In complete contrast, Denmark is also known for its twentieth-century Danish Modern design, now much collected.

A house brought to our attention by Alan Purchase, manager of the Brunschwig & Fils London showroom, and Bruno Garros, Brunschwig's export sales manager, is on the Costa Smeralda, in northeast Sardinia, Italy. Boasting a beautiful view, just in front

OPPOSITE

A bedroom vignette by Mark Gillette of Chester, England, combines *Timothy* woven plaid and *Liza* glazed chintz printed in England in gold-and-lavender honeysuckle on white.

ABOVE

An outstanding house in Madrid, Spain, was based on an architectural design by Cuban-born Emilio Terry, architect/designer and friend of many artists, such as Pablo Picasso and Salvador Dalí. The residence has been redecorated by designer Luis Alfonso Lopez Martinez. Shown here is the impressive sitting room with *Soleil* silk warp print in a damask pattern, used for the curtains, and *York* chenille on the sofa.

LEFT

Eugenio Garcia Cilleros, manager of one of the Brunschwig & Fils showrooms in Madrid, helped design this dining room in a holiday residence near the monastery of El Escorial in Spain. The walls and curtains are of *Glenrinnes Lodge* print. (See Alice Wiley's showhouse room on p. 160 for another use of *Glenrinnes Lodge*.) The chairs are covered in *Zambezi*.

of the marvelous Mortorio island, the site has been developed for some years by Luigi Vietti, one of Italy's most renowned architects. The house is owned by a couple who travel around the world, so their interior decorator Vanessa Tambelli of Arredare, in Milan, designed for them an eclectic medley of styles reflecting their travels. The furniture—which includes Italian, French, Chinese, and Indian pieces, with Moroccan and Japanese details added to the mix—brings a little part of the world into each corner of the house. Ideally suited to the project is *Clipper Ships,* a cotton print used in a bedroom as a coverlet. *Borghese* woven check silk and cotton is used for curtains.

Houston designer William Stubbs has worked far afield, in Russia, for some years. According to Michael Ennis in *Architectural Digest,* "He has decorated more than half a dozen jobs in the former Soviet republics, ranging from a two-story penthouse in Moscow to a castle outside Kiev," several of them using Brunschwig & Fils products. In renovating and decorating this caretaker's house on an estate in Ukraine, he used only local building materials. It became a local project and a "little jewel of a house," as Michael Ennis wrote. It was also a dry run for the larger manor house on the property. Much of the decoration involved "tactile, luxurious fabrics" to counteract the cold.

Brunschwig products are in use as far away as Jakarta, Indonesia. After ten years in the business of slotting qualified executives into lucrative

RIGHT
Brunschwig representatives Shozo and Yasuko Iida are photographed outside their new Tokyo showroom, which they call *Murray and Doug,* after Murray and Albert Douglas.

OPPOSITE
This watercolor by Murray Douglas is of a bedroom in a house in Sardinia. The bed cover is *Clipper Ships.* Curtains are of *Borghese* woven check from the Decortex collection.

William Stubbs of Houston designed this tiny caretaker's cottage. The background is *Forêt Foliage* wallpaper, its rich tapestry appearance in a cozy autumnal colorway setting the scene for rich, warm-toned textiles. (See *Forêt Foliage* in a green colorway in a watercolor of a children's playroom on p. 94 and used by Ginny Stine on p. 98.)

The living room in this photograph belongs to Gloria Zinnermann, managing director of Halogen International, the Brunschwig & Fils distributor for South Africa. The window overlooks the Good Hope Game Reserve. The fabrics used are a print *Le Zèbre* (this page) and *Zambezi gros point* (opposite).

In this East meets West–style living room, designer Marlene Tabalujan used a classic European toile *Parc de Vincennes*. The purple pillows and settee are of *Vivant* silk from the Jagtar collection, made in Thailand.

For this nicely restrained library/study, Jo and Ian Archibald (Decollo Design, Armadale, Victoria, Australia) used *Par for the Course* print on the cushions. The curtains in the all-beige room are of *Antares* woven polyester from Italy.

jobs, Marlene Tabalujan decided to pursue her longtime interest in interior design. She set up business for herself, importing exclusive fabrics, lamps, bed covers, cushions, and accessories. She offers design consultancy services for offices and residential work. "I am also promoting Indonesia by designing houses in Melbourne, Australia, using furniture from Indonesia," she says. In the photograph on the facing page, she has designed a living room that combines the decidedly Western *Parc de Vincennes* toile with an exotic splash of purple *Vivant* silk on a cushion.

By far the most photographs came in from Australia, where there is a rapidly growing market as people there become more interested in interior decoration. Australians are closer to Americans in their design style and way of life than Europeans, Africans, or Asians. Australia has the demand for the comfort and practicality typified in Brunschwig's upholstered furnishings and for serviceable, maintainable fabrics with plenty of visual appeal. The two

Stuart Rattle of Yarra, Victoria, Australia designed his own sitting room using *Venezia's Messina* on armchairs, beige-and-white *Crozon* check on the sofa with *Whitney* woven plaid, and *Spaniel* chenille for cushions. The designer says: "The *Crozon* check has given my sitting room a warm and luxurious feel. For some years I had thought the space didn't work, and I didn't enjoy the room. I am using the room all the time and entertaining clients at home. I really love it now!"

Australian Brunschwig & Fils showrooms—in the suburb of Armadale, near Melbourne, and in Woollahra, near Sydney—are flourishing.

The Australian firm of Thomas & Alexander Interiors, who maintain offices in Paddington, Queensland, and South Yarra, Victoria, have clients who live in a large Victorian house in a suburb of Melbourne. In it, the dining room had grand proportions but lacked decoration and soft furnishings. It had to be formal to work as a background for a fine collection of Chippendale furniture, English silver, and Australian Impressionist paintings, but it was also used regularly for Sunday lunch and more casual meals. Closing the gap between "grand" rooms and more relaxed rooms, the wallpaper *Kanchou* was selected for its color and vibrancy. Its chinoiserie design, seen on p. 132, became the inspiration for the fabrics and the rest of the room. The once-bland room, say the designers, thus became alive with the feeling of movement and color.

OPPOSITE

This bedroom designed by Thomas Hamel is in a beach house in an Australian fishing village. The look is right for simple vacation living, but it includes enough diverting personal details to make it successful. The handsome Scottish bed looks particularly attractive without drapery. The quilted bed cover is made from *Nanou Rockery* from the Cabanel collection (see it used also on pp. 55, 157, and 206).

ABOVE

Jo and Ian Archibald, of Decollo Design, work in Armadale, a suburb outside Melbourne, Australia. In this bedroom they used *Kininvie* toile for the curtains. (See p. 25 for a watercolor showing Linda Axe's use of the same fabric.)

OPPOSITE

This grand formal dining room was designed by Thomas & Alexander Interiors. The traditional furniture suits the chinoiserie floral background of *Kanchou* wallpaper. (See *Kanchou* used on the walls of the Brunschwig showroom in Manhattan on p. 37 and by John Banks on p. 187.)

TOP

Paddington designer John Glynn of the Design House, in Queensland, assembled this sun porch using faux bookcases he designed and made himself, backed with *Bibliothèque* wallpaper. The cushion covers, lamp shade, and tablecloth are of *Serenata* linen-and-cotton print, and the red fabric on the chair is *Alameda* twill. The tall, blue-and-white striped vase echoes the awning outside.

BOTTOM

Dean Sharpe and Neil McLachlan, of Revolution Interiors, designed this space in their Auckland, New Zealand, showroom using *Cathay* toile wallpaper. *Cathay* was chosen because of its timeless nature and exotic flavor. The shade of red complements French antiques displayed in the room. The contrast with the view into the adjoining hallway—with its bold black-and-white horizontal stripes—is dramatic.

8

Public Spaces
Hospitality, Health Care, and Contract Work

A growing part of the Brunschwig & Fils business is in the decoration of hotels, inns, clubs, and restaurants—known in the trade as hospitality. Brunschwig products have appeared in some of the world's best hotels. In Paris, the Bristol, the Hotel de L'Abbaye, and the Hotel des Grands Hommes have all used Brunschwig fabrics in their grand bedrooms. Visiting Geneva, Susannah Peardon saw, quite by chance, Brunschwig fabric used at the Beau Rivage. The Brunschwig agent Damiela Flamm, of Sofina, supplied material to the Swartzer Adler (Black Eagle) in Kitzbühel, Austria. In Puerto Rico, among various other rooms, the reception lounge at El Conquistador was decorated with blue-and-white *Majorca Ikat* print on white wicker furniture. In America, the Bellagio Hotel in Las Vegas, the Carriage House Inn in Atlanta, and the Sarasota Club can be added to an already-long list of public spaces using Brunschwig products.

Seen on the facing page, the Hotel Ritz, the premier hotel in Madrid, has several bedrooms designed by Jean Pierre Martel. All of them are intended to amaze you with a display of over-the-top extravagance.

Some hotels call upon "name" designers to decorate their extra-special suites or penthouse rooms but use designers who specialize in hospitality work for the regular rooms. If large

quantities of fabric or wallpaper from the Brunschwig collections are chosen, the designs may be modified with a different fiber content or perhaps fewer colors, but they always have to have the Brunschwig quality look.

Small, one-of-a-kind hotels and country inns use quantities more similar to those used in residential work, though everything employed in public spaces has to be able to stand up to heavy wear. If products are selected from the regular Brunschwig collections, they may be specially treated to be flame or spill resistant.

Loch Lomond Golf Club Arizona decorator Donna
Vallone, when working at Wiseman & Gale Interiors, in Scottsdale, Arizona, decorated a golf club called Loch Lomond, in Luss by Alexandria, Scotland. The club, opened by two Americans, has a number of bedrooms. In one suite—not only Donna's favorite, but the favorite of many guests—she used *Chinoiserie à l'Américaine* toile in charcoal and cream. This design was developed from a toile document that Brunschwig & Fils made for Mount Vernon, in Virginia. The Mount Vernon Board then requested that it be theirs exclusively, so the screens were destroyed. After some years (as the Mount Vernon retail store grew more important), they realized it would be profitable to sell adaptations of their holdings, including decorative fabrics, so the screens were remade allowing Brunschwig to include it and future adaptations in their collection. *Chinoiserie à l'Américaine* even outsells *Mount Vernon* toile, which was devised specially for Mount Vernon as a theme print. Donna Vallone now has her own firm, which includes contract work, and she continues to go to Scotland when new guest rooms are being added to the Loch Lomond Golf Club.

Donna Vallone decorated interiors for Loch Lomond, a golf club in Scotland. For a bedroom suite, she chose *Chinoiserie à l'Américaine* toile in charcoal and cream for bed hangings, walls, and in the bathroom. (This toile was also installed in a bedroom at Mount Vernon, seen on p. 32.) Watercolor by Murray Douglas.

The Inn at Little Washington

Little Washington, in Virginia, some sixty-five miles from Washington, D.C., predates the nation's capital. It is said—but not proved—that the tiny village was planned by George Washington as a youth while in the employ of Lord Fairfax. The 1900 building where the restaurant operates used to be a social hall, a general store, and an automotive garage before becoming an inn. Now it is considered one of the best inns and restaurants in America. The decor is by British theater designer Joyce Evans, who works closely with the owners. It aims for an unashamedly "Wow!" effect that is at the same time comfortable, if unexpected. Joyce Evans buys many of the fabrics from Brunschwig & Fils through the showroom in London. Many nice touches enhance the inn: the cooks in the custom-designed kitchen that combines old world with twenty-first-century technology wear very practical Dalmatian-print pants, in honor of the owners' dogs; a cow on wheels holds the cheese course tray; and upholstered dining-room chairs have handsome brass handles attached to their backs so they can be pulled out without dirtying the upholstery. The bedrooms are all different and equally imaginative. Even the inn's retail shop, which is across the street, is decorated to appeal to customers without competing with the merchandise.

OPPOSITE
Part of the eighty-seat dining room at the Inn at Little Washington, in Virginia, is a long, window-sided passage with a dramatically striped, tented ceiling. Banquettes upholstered in *Lille* tapestry sit against the wall. All the decor has a theatrical flavor because it was done by British stage-set designer Joyce Evans in conjunction with owner Patrick O'Connell. Curtains are of *Palampore* on the inside and *Palampore Rock Garden* facing the outside.

BELOW
This ballroom at the Inn at Little Washington is decorated with the suitably posh trompe l'oeil wallpaper *Tenture Flottante*.

The gift and antique store at the Inn at Little Washington is decorated to look like a home more than a shop. Here, Brunschwig's *Ascot* tartan wallpaper blends well with the pewter, Windsor chairs, and cozy fireplace.

A room in the retail store combines *Maize* wallpaper—a Nancy McClelland document— with *Chimayo* plaid curtains draped on a pole.

One of the guest bedrooms at the Inn at Little Washington is a duplex; a sitting room and bathroom are on the bottom floor, and the bed is in a sleeping loft above. The draped curtain is of *Rialto* woven imberline, and the walls of *Contarini* woven damask.

Yeshiva University's Stern College for Women

A very different hospitality project was given to New York designer Susan Aiello, of Interior Design Solutions, whose brief was to design a women's lounge and dining room for Yeshiva University's Stern College for Women, in Manhattan. As she wrote, "Living away from home, particularly in a big city like New York, can be stressful. Our client, a major university located in Manhattan, requested a dormitory lounge for young women that would create a sense of security and would encourage study, recreation, and informal gatherings."

The design for the project at Yeshiva University's Stern College for Women had to meet strict institutional guidelines for code compliance, value engineering, durability, and ease of maintenance, yet be sophisticated and tasteful enough to please a discriminating Board of Directors. Susan Aiello balanced a color palette that incorporated cool tones to evoke a sense of serenity and peace with warm ones that lift the spirit. Tables were movable so they could be employed individually or placed together for meetings or serving refreshments. "The completed lounge resembles a residential living room, the lobby of a fine hotel, or the lounge of an exclusive country club," says the designer. "The room is immensely popular with the students, staff, and members of the university's Board of Directors—and was completed well below budget!"

The design of offices and other professional spaces is called contract work, and some designers and architects specialize in this field. As with Susan Aiello's university job, they have to be aware of all the specifications needed to meet certain building codes. Brunschwig presents a Hospitality, Contract, and Health Care collection of fabrics each season using Trevira, a polyester that is processed to be washable and flame resistant but still luxurious. Fabrics in public spaces take a beating, and maintenance is key.

OPPOSITE TOP

This women's lounge and dining area at Yeshiva University's Stern College for Women, in Manhattan, was designed by Susan Aiello, of Interior Design Solutions, New York. On the blue sofas she used *Anna Maria* lampas. Other fabrics are *Echo* woven texture, *Aitken* woven texture, and *Valmy Lisere* stripe.

OPPOSITE BOTTOM

In this interior at Yeshiva University's Stern College for Women, Susan Aiello achieved a welcoming public area that does not look institutional. *Planter's Plaid* is the red check on the dining chairs.

The Residence at the Ritz-Carlton

In Washington, D.C., David Herchik and Richard Looman, of JDS Design, created some model rooms for the Residence at the Ritz-Carlton, Georgetown. This kind of project points out the fine line between residential and contract design. Not knowing the specific owner's tastes poses difficult problems. The rooms had to be luxurious, but sleek; traditional, yet modern; and have enough adornment to appear to be personal, yet appeal to a wide audience without offending anyone. Furnishings were from JDS Design's retail shop Hunters and Gatherers, in Kensington, Maryland, which is a stocking dealership (one of only three in the USA) for Brunschwig products, among other suppliers.

OPPOSITE

For one of several rooms in the model unit of the Residence at the Ritz-Carlton, in Georgetown, Washington, D.C., David Herchik and Richard Looman, of JDS Design, showcased a contemporary take on the Brunschwig & Fils aesthetic by using red-trimmed, black-and-white *West Indies* toile for curtains, dust ruffles, and walls in this bedroom but pairing it in a modern way with an undressed four-poster bed. The throw and chair upholstery are not Brunschwig but, amusingly, the well-known sporty Burberry plaid bought in London, for which the boots are an appropriate accessory.

RIGHT

Another bedroom designed by David Herchik and Richard Looman, of JDS Design, for the Residence at the Ritz-Carlton, in Georgetown, Washington, D.C., features the mirror-covered *Ducale* console. The bed upholstery is *Beaulieu* damask.

Fremont Elementary School   One of the most
exciting projects to come to our attention as we were working on
this book is the Fremont Elementary School in Mundelein, Illinois.
Using a "golden-oldie" design—one of the earliest print patterns
in Brunschwig's inventory—Chicago architect/designer Sanjay
Singhal gave it a bright, new, spirited flavor. The European design
Sun, Moon, and Stars dates from about 1790 to 1820 and was found
at Winterthur (see it on p. 49 used in Brooklyn Heights, New York,
in a traditional way). Sanjay Singhal looked at the fabric with
completely fresh eyes and employed it as the theme of the
impressive architectural project.

The school is set on a prairie site outside Chicago—
which is itself a town of innovative architecture and known for
its talented architects. On this project Sanjay Singhal was greatly
influenced by the architecture of Frank Lloyd Wright as well as
by Eero Saarinen's Crow Island School in Winnetka, Illinois, and
Perkin & Will's Perry Community Educational Village in Perry,
Ohio. Fifty different Brunschwig & Fils products were used in
project specifications. Apart from *Sun, Moon, and Stars* in various
significant color variations and textures, the designer selected the
rest of the fabrics and papers for their natural or organic themes:
leaves, coral, twigs, fiddlehead ferns, ladybugs, and so on. The
school runs from kindergarten to third grade, and each grade is
color coded: kindergarten is blue, first
grade is red, second grade is yellow, and
third grade is green. Awards for merit,
advancement, and special programs use
the same sun, moon, and star motifs. Even
the staff rooms utilize similar fabrics, and
Fiddlehead Fern woven was used as a tack-
surface material in offices, conference
rooms, and public spaces. Offices were

RIGHT

The floor-to-ceiling draperies in the
Fremont School library are a combination
of *Sun, Moon, and Stars* printed and
woven with *Frange Torse* trimming. Rolling
ottomans are upholstered in *Petit Point
Diamond*, *Ladybug* figured woven, and
Echo woven texture. The TV/VCR cart is
covered with *Sun, Moon, and Stars*
wallpaper and border.

TOP
The fabrics used in the gymnasium—stage curtains, backdrop, and ceiling panels—are all variations on the *Sun, Moon, and Stars* design but use different textures, some printed, others woven.

BOTTOM
The school's computer center has a deceptively grown-up look until you realize that all the tables and chairs are child-size. The students' chairs are covered in *Ladybug* figured woven; wall panels are of *Sun, Moon, and Stars* woven texture.

given Brunschwig's *Directoire Bouillotte* lamps, and the staff lounge has *Holloway Vase* lamps. When looking at the finished project, it seems such an obvious idea, but it took a forward-thinking designer to successfully make it look so happy and spontaneous.

Well-designed places for education, private and corporate offices, and professional spaces not only greatly affect our quality of life but also lift our spirits. Health-care projects also provide much-needed attractive and beneficial interiors for doctors' and dentists' offices, hospitals, nursing homes, spas, therapy and pain-management clinics, assisted-living spaces, and hospices for the growing number of older members of our population.

Retail stores come under the category of contract work. When we first started on this book and were searching for unusual uses of Brunschwig

Chicago architect Sanjay Singhal designed this first-grade classroom vignette using a scheme of *Sun, Moon, and Stars*—as a woven texture on the wall, as wallpaper and border on the TV/VCR cart, and as a cotton print and woven texture on cushions. Other cushions were made of *Gingko* cotton damask, *Trouville* chintz, and *Veranda* plaid with *Frange Torse* trimming. The rolling ottomans are covered in *Sun, Moon, and Stars* and *Echo* woven texture, *Bayberry* figured woven, *Veranda* plaid, and *Faux Bois* texture.

products, Murray Douglas came across a cake shop in Saratoga Springs. There, in the window of Mrs. London's Pastry Shop, was a background of the neoclassic wallpaper *Les Sylphides!* (*Les Sylphides* can be seen in all its glory in William Hulsman's landing on p. 191.) A shoe shop called Via Condotti, in Sydney, Australia, was just as unexpected.

ABOVE

Here is a shoe store in the Queen Victoria Building, Sydney, Australia, called Via Condotti, designed by Greg Natale. He used *Chanzeaux Tracery* wallpaper in a sage colorway for this modern setting.

RIGHT

Allendale, New Jersey, designer Virginia W. Smith decorated this executive office for Jane Elfers, the president of the department store Lord & Taylor. Ginny Smith used *Estancia* woven ikat in pink/green/gold on the chairs, *Bougival* cotton print for draperies, and *Spaniel* chenille in cinnabar color on the ottoman. The coffee table, end table, mirror, brackets, ottoman, and lamps—*Medici* urn, *Nippon* tole, *Demeter* floor lamp, *Artois Bouillotte,* and *Malta* lamp—are all from Brunschwig & Fils.

Part Three
Design Challenges

9

Showtime! Designer Showhouses

Interior decorators have a wealth of ideas, but their clients are not always ready to take risks. At showhouse presentations, though, designers have the opportunity to strut their stuff as outrageously as they wish. A chapter dedicated to this contemporary fund-raising drive is important, in that it clearly differentiates between rooms designed for show (as some clothes are designed purely for the runway) and rooms that are part of real life. Organized by hardworking committees that garner profit for deserving charities, these showhouses usually take place in a historically interesting large house, at a large house that is temporarily on the market, or in a design center. Most of the older houses have interesting, if idiosyncratic, architecture and odd-shaped rooms, which are both an inspiration and a challenge to designers. Visitors interested in interior design get a wealth of inspirational ideas as well as the fun of seeing amazing decor. Opening nights, for which patrons pay a hefty amount, are dressy, crowded, gala events. Visitors go to nibble hors d'oeuvres, drink champagne, scramble up and down narrow stairways to the attic rooms and even roof gardens, gawk across the velvet ropes, and be seen. Celebrities are present and journalists hover.

For designers, showhouses can be a two-edged sword because creating these rooms tends to be very expensive and you may draw a difficult room or a hall that no one stops to look at.

PREVIOUS SPREAD
Involve silk texture is an Indian silk-and-cotton ribbed ground fabric with a raised vermicelli design woven in.

OPPOSITE
This daringly colorful living room with a nod toward the "moderne" style was decorated for a 2002 Kips Bay Showhouse by New York designers Richard Ridge and Roderick Denault. They used six Brunschwig & Fils *Arthur* chairs and covered them with a broad spectrum of vivid colors selected from various Brunschwig solid-hued fabrics to get the effect. The ottoman, also by Brunschwig, is called *Patrick,* after Patrick Mongiello, president of Brunschwig & Fils.

Such projects can tie up a design office for weeks. All the specialty painters, mirror people, carpet layers, paperhangers, and upholsterers in town are busy with these deadlines. The designer then has to have someone man the room for the next three weeks. But showhouses can lead to new jobs, and they bring in publicity and contacts. Some designers may even sell the whole room to a client!

Not all showhouse rooms have to be big and spectacular. Some can be tiny, jewel-box spaces. A vignette on the facing page was created by Dennis Rolland for the Mount Vernon Hotel Museum and Garden Showhouse sponsored in New York by the Colonial Dames of America, who allot only a tiny space to each designer in their event. Dennis Rolland's exhibit showed the corner of a living room using a combination of *Nanou Rockery* wallpaper and *Aubin* cotton print for upholstery and curtains, different patterns but of a similar scale and coloring (also see pp. 182–183). *Aubin,* a late-eighteenth-century design, shows flower and fruit motifs, including pomegranates, which were a sign of fertility and often used on wedding quilts. The vignette is a petite and differently fabricated version of Diana Vreeland's famous living room—her "Garden in Hell," which was all crowded, intense reds. Not only the fabric but all the furnishings in the room by Dennis Rolland are Brunschwig's.

OPPOSITE

In this vignette for the Mount Vernon Hotel Museum and Garden Showhouse, Dennis Rolland used *Nanou Rockery* wallpaper, *Aubin* cotton print for upholstery and curtains, *Brittany* sofa and chair, *Atlante* table for books, a red *Queue* table, *Reggio* bracket, *Lausanne* lamp, and *Chau* floor lamp.

OVERLEAF

Boston designer Lindy Lieberman created this neutral-colored, calm, modern yet dateless reception living room for the 2002 Junior League Showhouse in Charleston. The effect is simple, but a wealth of details went into it. The background is *Seabury Stripe* wallpaper. Played against it are *Savannah* silk sheer curtains lined in *Multiraya* sheer, *Piedmonte* armless chairs and a *Wilcox* sofa all slip-covered in *Mirella* ottoman, a *Nantes* loose-seat chair covered in *Othello* damask, *Sunshine* silk woven for the table cover, *Watteau* silk taffeta and *Peau d'ane* silk on the pillows, plus two *Etienne* lamps, an *Aurora* lamp, and a Soane tall case—painted white. This doesn't count all the trimmings or the rest of the room!

San Francisco designer Alice Wiley decorated this living room using *Glenrinnes Lodge* print on chairs and drapery and *Deepdene* printed tapestry on the ottoman.

RIGHT

This living room, designed by Robert Kevin Cassidy of Plainville, Connecticut, was created for the 2001 Sarasota, Florida, Showhouse. As with many showhouse rooms, all the stops were pulled out in this large formal room. We zeroed in on a vignette that shows *Campanula* warp printed silk used for the draperies and to cover the ottoman. The *St. Charles* chair is upholstered in *Majeste* lampas.

BELOW

This library/living room, which Gregory Van Boven designed for the Boston Junior League 2003 Showhouse, shows a good use of the neutral beige-and-cream palette. In it are two *Wilton* chairs and a *Benson* ottoman covered in cream *Imperia* from the Venetia line. The pull-out shelf on the desk makes a practical piece of furniture, and in front of the plain mantelpiece, a beige-and-white fire screen is a nice use of a small screen for a summer decor.

Bogotá-born Juan Montoya studied architecture and painting in Colombia; environmental design at Parsons, in New York; and worked in Paris and Milan. Now he is a panel member of the National Endowment for the Arts, a trustee at Pratt, New York, and has a doctorate of fine arts from the New School in New York. The vast room he decorated at the Villa Maria for the Southampton showhouse is a multifunctional space, filled with a mélange of sophisticated materials. The carpet is of woven leather from India; hand-dyed shagreen finishes are on the tables, and all the furniture is designed by Montoya. Many of the art pieces are from his own collection. Among the fabrics used are *Paramo* woven texture in both *tabacco* color and *crudo, Astorga* woven texture in *crudo, Liso Jerez* woven texture in natural, *Indonesia* woven texture in *lino,* and *Luxor* woven sheer in eggshell. The whole room illustrates a superb way to reflect contemporary design.

OPPOSITE

New York designer Juan Montoya decorated this great room at the Villa Maria Showhouse in Southampton using all Brunschwig & Fils fabrics from the Gaston y Daniela collection in a palette of browns and naturals. Black-and-white punctuation is provided by the Montoya-designed furniture and fine-art pieces, much of it from his own collection. The effect is one of modern glamour.

RIGHT

In this spring 1998 Junior League of Louisville Showhouse, Beverly Sterry, of Beverly Beaver Design, took cherries as her theme and used *Cestas Ceritzas,* with its cherry print, in this kitchen-and-breakfast room. The café curtains are of green *Gazebo* checked sheer, and artificial cherries adorn them. The art, antiques, and accessories are from her husband, John Henry Sterry's, shop.

BOTTOM

Constance Paul, of Creative Designs, Castle Rock, Colorado, decorated this vignette of a bathroom/dressing room in the Grant Humphries Mansion (owned by the state of Colorado) for the Twenty-Fifth Showhouse of the Junior Symphony Guild in 2000. She used the all-over print *Benoa Contrefond* and *Round Hill* cotton print.

ABOVE

Melanie Cohrs designed this simple bedroom corner in neutral colors for the 1999 Charlotte Symphony Showhouse. The draped curtains are of *Watteau* silk trimmed with *Pondroon* taffeta to match the fabric on a chair. On the chaise is a modern vermicelli-style fabric called *Involve,* a silk texture, in *azur* (see pp. 152–153).

RIGHT

In the 2001 Villa Maria Showhouse in Southampton, New York, designer Matthew Patrick Smythe created this fairly traditional dining room but used an unexpected color palette. The bold, striped, upholstered walls are of *Chartres* woven stripe in *azul-verde* with *Nail Head* matte gimp trim. The apple green seat covers are of *Otoman Segura* with trimming and buttons of the same fabric in cream *crudo* coloring and custom embroidery worked by Interior Embroidery, New York. The pillows are covered in *Eden* embroidery in nutmeg; the window seat is upholstered in *Sparta* texture in *gris azur;* and the Roman shades are of beige *Vienna* sheer.

A showhouse with a practical-over-posh theme was held at the Center for Family Development Showcase at Our Lady of Bethesda retreat in Maryland, which benefits the family counseling center there. Rather than being a "show-off" exercise in opulence, the showhouse consisted of a series of rooms for ordinary people—"inventive ideas on a budget." All the rooms were small with clunky radiators, dated casement windows, and low ceilings. Richmond, Virginia, designer Kate Oliver said, "If you have to do chores, you might as well be surrounded by happy things." She was inspired by Brunschwig & Fils' *Ironing Bored* wallpaper, which is a whimsical and charming period piece of a woman pressing clothes. A border that can go with it is *On Line,* which shows washing hanging on a line. The fabrics in varying designs of white and salmon complement the walls. Both ironing boards—one for a grown-up and one for a child—have coordinating covers. The curtains are *Pekin Cuadros, a* cotton-and-linen print from the Gaston y Daniela collection. The sheer shade is of *Tic-Tac* woven plaid trimmed with *Menuiserie* wood-mold fringe.

Richmond, Virginia, designer Kate Oliver, of Oliver Design Associates, was inspired by a kitchen/laundry-room theme wallpaper called *Ironing Bored* when she designed a space for the Center for Family Development Showcase in Bethesda, Maryland. A wallpaper border to go with it is *On Line,* and the rest of the room carries out the color scheme, even to the two ironing boards.

Winnetka, Illinois, designer Susan Schmidt decorated this pretty blue-and-white bedroom for the Infant Welfare Society of Chicago Homes and Gardens Showhouse in 1997. She used *Highland Thistle* for the dust ruffle and valence, *New Cholet* plaid for the table skirt and trim on ruffles, *Pompeian* stripe in a custom color, *Peaweed* cotton print in pale green for the canopy lining and coverlet, *Amalfi* moiré in fern green for the bench fabric, and a *Maywood* urn lamp.

OPPOSITE

A vignette of Gregory Van Boven's bedroom for the Massachusetts showhouse shows a use of the perennial favorite *Coligny* in pink and green (see it in this coloring in the Brunschwig New York showroom on p. 215 and in a New York apartment in a special coloring on p. 200).

ABOVE

In this traditional family room for the Junior League of Hartford Showhouse, Sal Modifica, of Modifica Interiors, used *Ode to Spring* for drapery with *Bremen* sheer undercurtains. A *Bedford Quilt* is on the chair with dog heads on the arms (echoing the dog on the mat) with *Nail Head* matte gimp trimming. The wallpaper is *Seabury Stripe*. On the chair in the foreground is *Danielle* figured ottoman, and *Chandler* figured woven is on sofa. One cushion is made from woven ribbons, a nice design idea to help coordinate colors in a room. Also in the room is a *Monmouth* lamp and a *Portsmouth* table.

10

Designers' Dilemma:
Choices, Choices

Notes on Creating and Re-Creating a Home

Murray Douglas has been intimately involved with the workings of the interior-decorating business over the years. As she says, she has used her own spaces—her office, her apartment in New York, her house in upstate New York, and a cottage in St. Croix—as laboratories to experiment with rooms, furnishings, and fabric.

———

MURRAY: *Ten years ago I wrote about "the starter apartment," or how young people starting out can decorate from scratch. Those principles still work. When we bought a historic nineteenth-century cottage in St. Croix, it was similar to starting over. The former owner left beds and rattan headboards, but no chests of drawers and no bedside tables. A caned, scrolled settee from Sri Lanka was the only centerpiece of the living room. Fortunately, my mother, who had just given up her house, had several comfortable slip-covered chairs, a daybed to become a sofa, a family portrait, a three-paneled louvered screen, and a medium-size, two-part bookcase-secretary to provide height, display shelves, and storage. The screen created an entrance hall.*

Our major expense was for a sisal rug, which anchored the sitting area. Fortunately, the floor needed only simple refinishing. I found a local seamstress who

OPPOSITE

Murray and Albert Douglas's bedroom in the country, designed by Nan Heminway, owes its delightful femininity to the *Emma's Ribbons* glazed chintz bed hangings and headboard. The design came from a nineteenth-century scrap from the Brunschwig Archive. The hangings are suspended directly from the ceiling, giving the effect of a four-poster bed. The red-and-white check on chair and seat pad add to the room's comfortable, country look.

In summer Murray Douglas uses *Mrs. Delany's* seats and backs. It is an engineered print with a back, front, and arm covers to make into chair slipcovers. Sheer curtains catch summer breezes. Shelves are filled with Murray's heirloom Thompson family armorial 1835 china. On the wall are framed prints found on a grand tour by Murray's great-uncle, Benjamin Comegys, of Philadelphia.

LEFT

The original document from the Brunschwig Archive is a slipcover embroidered by Mrs. Mary Delany herself in the eighteenth century. She was a formidable hostess, knew everyone of importance, and in her diary wrote about rushing round removing "loose covers" when guests were due so as to reveal the more precious stuff underneath.

In Murray and Albert Douglas's country house, the decor is changed seasonally, with *Tuscan* texture on vinyl wallpaper remaining constant. This winter arrangement shows *Helen* striped taffeta curtains and *Filoli Tapestry* cotton-and-linen print on a barrel-back armchair. Dining-chair slipcovers are *Marion strié* texture. The shelves hold English Staffordshire and French nineteenth-century china in winter. Even the ribbon around the neck of a bust of Pauline Borghese (Napoléon's sister) on the mantel is changed to complement the scheme.

made slipcovers and cushions out of a blue-and-white Brunschwig print called Benoa. *We filled empty corners with potted palms. For decoration, my blue-and-white Spode reproduction china was the perfect tropical solution—easy to clean, and rain and mildew proof! Hurricane globes lit a skirted table under a family mirror. No curtains were needed, as louvered shutters controlled light and allowed air circulation, so thankfully, air conditioners were unnecessary.*

Later we purchased a reproduction four-poster bed from the St. Croix Landmarks Society made by Baker furniture. This was the master bedroom furniture. A washable dimity made the coverlet, and mosquito net the canopy. A simple table with skirt and oval mirror became a dressing table.

We gradually acquired tables, chairs, and bureaus from local antique dealers and auctions and from friends' storerooms. All in all, it was printed fabrics that pulled the house together and turned picnic tables into semiformal dinner settings, lit romantically with kerosene lamps and hurricane globes.

Now, having decided to give up our house in the tropics, I am looking to simplify living in our New York apartment and our upstate house. So, instead of "starter" decorating, I, along with many others I have spoken to, am dealing with what to do with apartments and houses when the children have grown and left home and the family is reduced in size.

With a son in Seattle, I finally have a place for a large family Persian Feraghan rug, which is too dark for our ground-floor brownstone apartment, so I will send it to him. A new, light green carpet will brighten our big New York living room. Its balloon silk-striped curtains will go. There will be a fresh color scheme to integrate the rug, blue-and-white Canton china, and new printed linen slipcovers for the sofa and arm chairs.

In our country house, which we visit most weekends, we have invented a fuel-saving routine that begins after the first frost. We close down the heat in the old schoolhouse wing, turn off the water, and keep the doors to that area closed.

To compensate for no big sitting area, we have turned the dining room into a living/dining area. Two leaves of the table are removed, and the table is moved away from the fireplace and closer to a big window. It now seats six—eight at a squeeze. Around the chimneypiece are several arm chairs, and a settee that can seat three comes down from the attic. Thus, six people can comfortably have drinks and dine in the cozy and cheerful space. The setting is enhanced with winter striped curtains, which can be closed, and warm, salmon-colored slipcovers on the chairs add to the seasonal change from summer sheers and blue-and-white dining-chair covers.

Last summer at our Shaker Museum antiques fair, I spotted a needlepoint rug with a chicken motif coinciding with my chicken paintings collection. Since we share our porch in winter as a plant conservatory, the rug suggested a seasonal change, accomplished with slipcovers and cushion changes and a long table skirt for the round dining table. With these changes the house as a whole seems larger rather than diminished. The traffic pattern has changed as well. If we have a big party, on goes the heat in the wing, the doors open, and the porch becomes a serving bar to the living room—with fireplace working.

Most fortuitously, when we added to the schoolhouse, there was a chance that my mother would come to live with us . . . so we added a bedroom and bath on the ground floor. That phase didn't happen, but we are now so grateful for the resulting no-stairs bedroom.

———————————

LEFT

This photograph shows the porch of Murray's country house in the summer. It combines *Adirondack Patchwork,* made in India of bright madras cotton as a tablecloth, with a cotton print *Les Chenapans*—"the naughty boys"—with yellow ground used as a seat pad that converts a folding campaign bed into a settee. *Les Chenapans* with a blue ground is used for cushions and dining-chair seat pads. *Potomac* linen check in red and white are accent cushions. The rug is from Greece. A collection of spongeware fills the shelves.

BOTTOM

This watercolor by Murray Douglas shows a detail of her porch in its summertime decor.

OPPOSITE

The winter decor of Murray and Albert Douglas's country house includes a collection of chicken pictures. Shelves are filled with chickens and roosters from Mexico and Santa Fe. The cotton print *Flew the Coop* on cushions and table is perfect for the room, enhanced by solid-yellow seat pads and green sofa pad and with the colorful *Mandira Quadros* woven plaid (see p. vi).

CHIPPY: *Slipcovers are a prerequisite in the Irvine house. Every summer each chair and sofa in our country ballroom gets a white cotton slipcover—we used to call them dust covers or loose covers in England. Be sure to use preshrunk fabric because slipcovers always look more genteel if they have just a little casual looseness. All the small cushions are then covered in a variety of green toile patterns. The slipcovers protect the upholstery from summer's bright sunlight and also look good against the greenery of potted plants. It transforms the room and lifts the spirits for dreamy "Smiles of a Summer Night" dances.*

Some things we've learned along the way:

❋ *A house or apartment can be replanned for changes in lifestyle without the agony of moving.*

❋ *It helps to have good storage space for seasonal furnishings: slipcovers, folding furniture, extra china for wall and tabletop changes.*

❋ *Edit—give away or sell objects that stay in boxes all year or that you just don't like.*

❋ *If you have attic space, keep the objects you can't use for the children or grandchildren to discover. They are more apt to take an object they have found themselves.*

❋ *If you have given away a piece of furniture or an object, don't ask for it back unless you suspect that your house may become a museum after you've gone!*

❋ *China that you seldom or never use makes a great display and can become a focus—combined with a room with many books, used on shelves, or arranged on the wall above a chest. And it doesn't fade!*

❋ *Use a professional decorator to help you, and it will save you money in the long run.*

Murray Douglas painted a watercolor of her friend Jane Hanna's kitchen, where *Hancock* woven plaid was used for the seat cushions and the cherry-printed fabric *Cestas Ceritzas* was used for the window seat. This immediately dressed up the whole room. Murray added the bowl of cherries for fun.

Upholstery

If you are dealing with upholsterers, it is a good idea to know how to use upholstery nail heads correctly. Nails and gimp were traditionally used because they were neater, less obvious, and easily applied. If no appropriate gimp exists, use a thin fabric, such as a satin, so a double welt doesn't look too thick and clumsy. Single welts against the wood frame must be hand sewn, not glued (as double welts are), and may increase the cost of upholstery work, but this will give a neater, slimmer appearance.

Traditionally, European furniture was arranged against the walls and was not placed, as today, in the open. A less-expensive fabric was used on the backs of chairs, since it wouldn't be seen. This led to the practice of using checked linen or other less-formal and less-expensive fabrics on the backs of chairs. That custom is often followed today; indeed, we find it charming, even when, on dining-room chairs, the back is usually

Julie Stander of Houston, Texas, designed this children's room for a family in Baton Rouge, showing that even for the young, china displayed in shelves can be a decorative element. She used the print *En Plein Air,* both wallpaper and fabric, combined with *Tobago* check and *Carolina* sheer curtains.

A dining room for the
Zurbrugg Showhouse in
Moorestown, New Jersey, that
was designed by Audrey Shinn
tells a story with its trompe
l'oeil painting by John Albright
of an open door with an old-
fashioned-looking child with
two cats and the corner of a
classical pediment. Curtains
in *Phoebe Ann* silk plaid in
raspberry, aqua, and peach
match the chair *backs*—
because that's what you see
first on entering today's dining
rooms. On these chairs solid-
colored *Baldwin* texture is on
the fronts.

In Murray Douglas's New
York office, the oval-backed
slipper chair to the right is
upholstered with *Dancing
Ladies* cotton print. The two
differently sized design motifs
are correctly centered on the
back and seat and held in
place with *Nail Head* gimp,
which imitates brass-headed
upholstery nails.

seen first. However, in the dining room designed by Audrey Shinn seen on the facing page, she has faced up to the fact that nowadays we *do* see the backs of dining-room chairs far more than the fronts because chair seats are either tucked into the table or people are sitting on them. She has put the more decorated fabric deliberately on the back and the plainer material on the front.

A large-scale or complex print is often shown to better advantage on a chair or sofa than made into curtains. This is because the fabric is stretched out smoothly so that the full design is shown. In curtains the print is bunched up in gathers most of the time. Placing the design on a piece of furniture, and on a valance, is a crucial decision that should be made with the help of a professional designer. Even the height of a seat pad can be consequential, as one of Murray's friends discovered to her cost, when she, on her own, got it wrong.

Using an interior designer has many advantages. It will save you time searching not only for fabric, trim, and wallpaper but also furniture, antiques, accessories, and ordinary things like household linens and everyday appliances. Designers have their own lists of contacts, skilled artisans, and sources. In the long run, it is more than cost effective because there is less danger of making expensive mistakes.

Some fabrics are very expensive, but small amounts can be used on cushions or, as here, on a slipper chair. This chair, upholstered in *Fragole* brocade, belonged to Zelina Brunschwig, who gave it to Ross Francis, the design director at Brunschwig for many years. It shows how even small amounts of costly fabric can add elegance to a room.

Breaking the Rules   Skilled designers occasionally break rules. The well-established way to design a scheme is to have several solid-textured fabrics and one or two prints that pick up the solid colors. As a rule, one of the prints will be a small all-over, or a small check or stripe, and the other a larger, more complex design so that plenty of contrast exists between the two. Yves Taralon, designing a bedroom in France, chose to use two different documentary designs, but of similar scale, coloring, and stripe formations—and in close proximity. The result as seen in the illustrations on pp. 182–185 is startling but

PREVIOUS SPREAD AND THIS PAGE
Skilled designers can break the rules. French designer Yves Taralon designed this bedroom for the home of William Berthe, head of Brunschwig's Paris showroom. He used two similarly scaled and colored prints in close proximity—*Villeroy,* a *toile de Nantes* with twisted stripes, and *Wickham,* an English documentary print on linen with stripes—and it works! *Crozon* check is used on the table, and *Butterscotch* plaid check on the bed.

intriguing. *Villeroy,* a *toile de Nantes* documentary print, has a twisted column forming the stripes. *Toiles de Nantes* were more countrified than the sophisticated toiles de Jouy, being larger in scale and bolder. They usually incorporated heavy vertical, undulating, decorated stripes, as this does, with foliage designs between that have dominating, large, decorative flower motifs. *Wickham* was developed from a document in the Brunschwig and Fils Archive. It is equally bold, similar in scale, and designed around the same period but has straight stripes. (See p. 157 for Dennis Rolland's smaller-scale version of two competing patterns at his vignette at the Hotel Mount Vernon Showhouse.)

Specialty painting and fantasy finishes became so overused—and misused—in the 1980s that afterward they went by the wayside for a while. Now, interesting new, personal examples of them can be seen cropping up in interiors, such as in the Audrey Shinn showhouse room on p. 180. In a real house in New Jersey, designers Carl D'Aquino and Francine Monaco of D'Aquino/Monaco commissioned Marguerite MacFarlane to paint the risers of a staircase with a boat-filled seascape that has a surprising, dramatic effect. This kind of painting gives a way of customizing an interior space. Wallpapers and wallpaper borders can also look effective used on the risers of stairs.

OPPOSITE

For the Harrisburg Symphony Showhouse, in Lebanon, Pennsylvania, decorator Ron Shepler designed a bedroom using *Bangalore,* a printed indienne in *verde rojo* (green/red) for the quilted bedspread and pillows. To line the canopy, he chose *Liso Jerez* woven in *pizarro* (green) and *teja* (red). This is an inexpensive Gaston y Daniela cotton broadcloth, but it has a sumptuous effect here—and could be interpreted in many colorways. The malachite green English wallpaper is called *Tuscan* texture on vinyl.

ABOVE

In this master-bedroom vignette from the Atlanta Symphony Showhouse, John S. Banks used *Placido* woven plaid in raspberry and blue for a table skirt, tailoring it so that the large check pattern does not get distorted by being on the bias but instead forms inverted pleats that hang from a circular top. On a table like this, it is important also to have a glass top to take the brunt of spills and dirt. The wallpaper is *Kanchou. Watteau* silk is used for bed hangings and curtains with *Rêve de Papillon* fringe and tiebacks.

M DOUGLAS

11

Climbing the Walls
Using Wallpaper

Wallpaper can give color and drama to a room. It can have reflective qualities, as in silvery tea paper, which was used to line tea-packed crates in the eighteenth century. Using borders in place of cornices, friezes, or dados, it can give architectural strength. It can expand the room by giving the impression of space, by using trellis-style papers, or make a room have bandbox neatness with tiny borders—plain paper, braid, gimp, or ribbon—outlining doors, windows, skirting boards, crown molding, and even crisscrossing ceilings. Some wallpapers with a "growing" movement can give height to a room.

Traditional, large-scale patterns in strong colors are used in entrance halls to give a sense of parade as one walks through the space, especially if the pattern continues up the staircase to the landing floor, but such wallpapers might be too busy in a room where more time is spent. On p. 191 can be seen the upstairs landing of a grand entrance hall William Hulsman designed using the neoclassic arabesque wallpaper *Les Sylphides.* Another arabesque wallpaper is *Aurora,* adapted from a documentary found at the Phelps-Hatheway House, in Suffield, near Hartford, Connecticut. One of the Brunschwig & Fils American wallpaper printers was on holiday visiting Kylemore Abbey, a Victorian Gothic castle in Connemara County, Galway, when he saw a great treatment of a reception room there using *Aurora* wallpaper, which his company had printed! He was as thrilled as we were to realize the international reach of our wallpaper collection.

Precious ornamental patterns work wonderfully in powder rooms. Because these are tiny spaces, it is possible to

OPPOSITE

In Kansas City, Joye Adamson, a Brunschwig & Fils independent distributor and interior designer at Stoney Broke Ltd., used *Damietta* panel wallpaper in a showhouse oval dining room that inspired Murray Douglas to paint this watercolor.

ABOVE

Westport, Connecticut, designer Audrey Morgan decorated this Park Avenue foyer using the novelty circus wallpaper *A Tribute to John S. Churchill.*

OPPOSITE

Boston designer William Hulsman decorated a grand entrance hall using *Les Sylphides* wallpaper. This shows the upstairs landing with a central table and chairs. A *Scroll Loveseat* is under the window. The curtains are of *Clarendon* moiré imberline.

use costly and glamorous papers such as the silver and gold tea papers that might be too fancy for a larger space.

Toile de Jouy designs give warmth and comfort to many rooms, but to bedrooms in particular, as they imitate fabric-covered walls. Considering their current popularity, Murray Douglas predicts a return to more patterned walls.

Novelty wallpapers are fun to use in small areas such as tiny halls or bars. One such is *A Tribute to John S. Churchill,* seen on this page and also in a hall in Belgium on p. 116.

Contrary to some assumptions, plain walls are not always the best background for paintings and artwork, unless you want the space to resemble an art gallery. A deep-colored, richly patterned wallpaper can be a wonderful foil for good, gilt-framed paintings. Well-chosen wallpapers can greatly enhance an art collection.

For heavily traveled areas, Brunschwig presents a collection of washable textured vinyl wallpapers filling a much-needed niche.

Most wallpaper installations need a lining paper first. Fabric can and should be backed with canvas or paper to make it easier to hang on, and also to remove from, walls. Canvas or muslin backing is a must for expensive papers and scenic papers.

Wallpapers with trellis motifs come in wonderful variations. *Sea Island* trellis, as seen in Lindy Leiberman's reception pavilion, gives an open-air vacation flavor. *Treillage de Bambou* is suave, with a touch of Far Eastern places. A trellis that brings a smile is *Frog Treillage,* mentioned on p. 215.

OPPOSITE

Boston designer Lindy Lieberman, of Living Spaces, decorated this reception pavilion for the Junior League Showhouse of 1998 using light-colored, textured upholstery—very sensibly, so the fabric will not bleach out in the sun. The accessories—mercury glass, drinks tray, globe astrolabe, mirrored coffee/drinks table—work well against the *Sea Island* trellis wallpaper, which sets the mood of the space.

TOP

Boston designer Laura Glen created this front parlor for the 2001 Quincy showhouse. She used brown *Gallier Diamond* wallpaper and *Scarlett* stripe from the Verel de Belval collection.

BOTTOM

In this showhouse in Quincy, Massachusetts, designer Gerald Pomeroy used the neoclassic wallpaper *Le Bain de Paon* in this formal dining room, together with *Linen Moiré* texture.

Seen as a watercolor at the beginning of this section in a dining room, and in a bathroom and a bedroom on this page, *Damietta* panel wallpaper—despite its size and dramatic effect—has a versatile appeal. It can be used with its own crown border and a narrow border. The design is a French block print from about 1800 to 1805, and it came from the Musée du Papier Peint de Rixheim, Alsace. A large-scale design of a stylized palm tree, the original coloring had red, leafy blossoms springing from the top and a feathery green trunk wrapped in spiraling white bands alternating with dusty green sprays of white yucca set in treelike form. Daisies and foliage surround the base. Brunschwig & Fils offers it in three colorways. *Damietta* panel wallpaper was even hung in the Governor's Mansion, Columbia, South Carolina, where designer David Ogburn chose it for a private dining room.

Murray Douglas has noted that over the last few years wallpaper has become less patterned and contrasted; it is still a background, but more subtle. A marked preference for *striés* (which imitate paint effects), stripes, tiny textured repeats, and straw effects prevails.

OPPOSITE TOP

Fredericksburg, Virginia, decorator Elaine Thomas, of Impressions Ltd., used *Damietta* panel wallpaper with its palm tree in a delightful way in this 1997 showhouse bedroom by putting it not only on the walls but also using it with *Chartwell* jaspé stripe in a dramatic way on the ceiling. The bedspread is of *Hameau* taffeta plaid.

OPPOSITE BOTTOM

Mark and Eden Cross, of M & E Cross, in Palm Coast, Florida, used *Damietta* panel wallpaper in this bathroom for the 2000 Dream House Interior Design Competition. (See another use of this on p. 188.) A floral basin is set into the bombé-shaped vanity of empress green marble. The side wallpaper is *Bourbon.*

ABOVE

Designer Carol Lynn Forman of Gates Mill, Ohio, decorated this attractive attic suite using *Tipperary* wallpaper on the side walls and the ceiling; cozy, green, wall-to-wall carpeting to tie in with the green-and-white bed cover; and *Walnut Tree* print for curtains and the upholstered top of a wicker bench.

Naturally white horsehair made and embroidered in France shows the change from caterpillar to butterfly in this design called *Metamorphosis.*

Naturally black horsehair is embroidered in France with feathers of multicolored, silk thread.

For the fall 2004 collection, a bedroom designed by Bill Walter was given tall folding screens covered in *Bamboo Grove* tea paper with a shimmering silver background. On the bed in the foreground is *Lucky* figured woven, which shows clover leaves—with the occasional four-leaf one—designed by New York decorator Thomas Jayne.

Screens

Another good use for wallpaper is on screens. *Damietta* panel would be an excellent choice for a tall screen, the sort that might be used in a formal dining room to shield a door leading to the kitchen or butler's pantry. A plainer wallpaper can be used to back a decorative screen that is full of personal memorabilia—such as snapshots or postcard collections—to be used in a bedroom, bathroom, or office. Annell Slack, the head of the San Francisco Brunschwig & Fils showroom, came up with a neat idea. She has an office lined with *Cathay* toile, and she had made a matching, three-way toile screen of just the right height to mask computer paraphernalia on her desk.

Screens, like walls, can be upholstered with fabric. Classic screens are covered with dark green baize or felt, usually held in place with upholstery nails. More imaginative screens can do a lot for a room, adding height, counteracting a particularly heavy piece of furniture, or as in design director Albert Sardelli's New York apartment, acting as a floor-to-ceiling room divider.

A really precious screen could be covered with one of the magnificent real horsehair fabrics from France. Only twenty-three inches wide—the length of a horse's tail—they come in natural plain, mixed, and woven colors. Two especially stand out because they are also embroidered. *Metamorphosis* is natural ivory–colored, embroidered with curlicues of matching cords, which are interspersed with delicate, silk-embroidered insects. The other, *Ruffle Your Feathers,* is a natural

black horsehair scattered with feathers embroidered in muted, multicolored, silk thread. Either one would look fabulous on a screen. San Francisco interior designer James Hunter, of the Wiseman Group, decorated a jewel box of a powder room using inset panels of *Metamorphosis* on the walls. He also used *Ruffle Your Feathers* on a bench in a music room. In Houston, an office building for a bank had a whole bank of elevators lined in horsehair. Of course these materials are very expensive, so they have to be used in small quantities and with discrimination.

12

Curtains for You, Baby
Grand to Simple

Curtains serve many purposes: for privacy, for warmth, to soften the hard edges of a window, to prevent light from coming in, to prevent light from damaging precious rugs and upholstery, to allow a controlled amount of light in, to pull a room together, and to add purely decorative exuberance.

Curtains (sometimes referred to as "drapes," though not at Brunschwig) were made by upholsterers in the seventeenth, eighteenth, and nineteenth centuries who were in many ways like the decorators of today. The "chief agent," the main boss—usually an upholsterer and curtain maker—called in the various skilled tradesmen, which the *London Tradesman* in the eighteenth century described as "Cabinet-Makers, Glass-Grinders, Look-Glass Frame-Carvers, Carvers for Chairs, Testers and Posts of Beds, the Woolen-Draper, the Mercer, the Linen-Draper, several Species of Smiths, and a vast many Tradesmen of other mechanic Branches." In a great house, the most money was spent on curtains and bed hangings, even more than on the actual furniture. Many of these elaborate bed hangings have survived from the eighteenth century—many fewer from earlier, and fewer of the actual window curtains because they take the brunt of damaging sunlight. However, drawings and paintings exist today that can be studied. English mid-twentieth-century decorator John Fowler (of Colefax & Fowler) made a point of researching English and, especially, French curtains. He resurrected the disciplined elegance of the swags and jabots of eighteenth- and early-nineteenth-century curtains. Much of this elegance had been lost by the end of the

OPPOSITE

The New York firm Irvine & Fleming created these beautifully constructed curtains of *Castets* silk damask in straw color for the drawing room of an elegant Palm Beach house designed by architect Maurice Fatio. They are trimmed with *Complement* inset braid and *Othello* cording. The upholstery in the room—just showing at the bottom of the photograph—is the large-scale glazed chintz *Le Lac,* a longtime favorite (also mentioned on p. 32).

late nineteenth century in both Europe and America, as industry brought wealth to many, fabric became cheaper, and ostentatious overcurtains, undercurtains, innercurtains, blinds, and portieres indiscriminately swamped the rooms of the newly rich. Fowler, who in his mature years worked for many National Trust properties, designed curtains for a number of well-proportioned London terrace houses drawing on brilliant, but formal, Regency styles often dubbed Mayfair curtains. Really gorgeous, glamorous curtains are still impressive and work well in high-ceilinged, architectural rooms.

Professional-looking curtains take time, skill, and an expert upholstery workroom with industrial sewing machines and long tables for cutting. They need lining—which can be plain or printed—interlining flannel and/or blackout lining, trimmings (braids, fringes, or beading), and various specialized stiffeners for valances. Designers have to discover and use the best workrooms they can.

If a complex print is used for curtains, some of the design may get lost in the gathers. In that case the valance works best when partially smoothed out, so that the design can be read. The ideal valance should look as if it just happened naturally—as if held by invisible classical cherubs! It should never look overworked. Placing the design on the curtains and the valance is as crucial as placing a design on furniture.

The fabric that designer Arlene Reilly chose to use for curtains is a popular linen-and-cotton print called *Sultan of Gujarat.* Brunschwig & Fils had for some time wanted to make a fabric adaptation from a carpet design. An exotic pattern on a rug in the Henry Francis du Pont collection at the Winterthur Estate caught our attention. The center field of the rug contains a large, diamond-shaped medallion with serrated edges and four marine scenes

OPPOSITE

New York decorator William Kulp designed these formal curtains for Ross and Mac Francis's high-ceilinged Manhattan apartment using *Cyrus* and *Meudon* warp printed taffetas as alternating swags on the valance. The chair is covered in a special color of *Coligny* glazed chintz.

ABOVE

Bernardsville, New Jersey, designer Arlene Reilly created these dramatic curtains using a nice treatment of the linen-and-cotton print *Sultan of Gujarat*. The pattern was adapted from an Indian rug.

OVERLEAF LEFT

Avon, Colorado, decorator Eddy Dumas, of Worth Interiors, designed this pleasant morning room with its tea table near a window. He used a favorite print, *Fabriano,* for these alluring curtains. *Fabriano* is a print that can be gathered into curtains without losing the integrity of its design.

OVERLEAF RIGHT

For a client who lives in a small Victorian villa in the suburb of Toorak, Australia, Stuart Rattle designed curtains using longtime favorite *Fabriano*. This detail shows how he trimmed them with *Complement* brush fringe and *Complement* cord on tape in chartreuse.

Louise and Jeffrey S. Quéripal, of Quéripal Interiors, designed this vignette of a yellow bedroom showing a clever use of the diamond-shaped design of *Maria Christina* blue-and-white print from the Gaston y Daniela collection and a variation on goblet pleats. The pleats are lined in solid blue *Callaway* chintz texture, and a blue ribbon effect holds the valance pleats.

in the corners. In each vignette was a sailing ship with two oversize and strangely dressed people. A naked man in the water indicated a ferocious sea monster. Now known to have been made in India, this rug is one of only nine such that survive today. A miniature painting entitled *The Death of Bahdur Shah, Sultan of Gujarat, While Visiting the Portuguese Fleet* has a similar scene. Whether the scene shows Portuguese sailors outside the Indian port of Goa, which in the seventeenth century was a Portuguese colony, or has an even more mystical interpretation, this design was the inspiration for Brunschwig's *Sultan of Gujarat.* One of the designers at the Brunschwig Studio worked from photographs—no possibility of borrowing the actual precious rug existed. The best layout for the use of the design on upholstered pieces as well as for curtains was carefully researched, and all the colors were drawn from Oriental, Indian, and Persian carpets. Arlene Reilly's curtains, especially the placement of the design on the valance, are skillfully accomplished.

One of the most-used ongoing fabrics is *Fabriano,* a design based on a document from the Brunschwig Archive in the form of a late-nineteenth-century padded coverlet of peach taffeta brocaded with silk and silver thread. An identical coverlet was found in Italy, so it is possibly Italian in origin. It was adapted into a linen-and-cotton print and a moiré print (eliminating the silver thread effect), both of which work successfully because of the design's proportions and easy-to-live-with design. (See *Fabriano* on pp. 202–203, used by Eddy Dumas and also by Stuart Rattle.)

Blinds can give a lift to a mundane room. In a New York kitchen with an exposed brick wall, designer William Kulp made blinds of the indienne

Colombo—the same print Diana Vreeland used for her "Garden in Hell" drawing room. Sheer café curtains give privacy but let in light, as can be seen in Beverly Beaver Sterry's kitchen on p. 163. Austrian and balloon shades are variations for more formal rooms.

Curtains nowadays get more and more simple; in some cases they have become just sheets of fabric slung over a pole or have a heading through which a pole is slotted. With the abundance of beige, cream, and neutral rooms, less danger of bleaching from the sun exists, so curtains—if used at all—can be unlined. Murray Douglas likes more color on walls, but less fabric in quantity and pattern in a room. Windows look good with simple curtains or none at all. She also likes lots of pattern all over using the same fabric on the wall and furniture and prefers classic styling and less Victorian clutter.

LEFT

In this vignette for the Catasauqua showhouse at the Biery House, designer V. Milou MacKenzie used 100 percent Trevira *Placido* woven plaid in sorrento and gold for the curtains and upholstery. *Mariella* stripe was used for the ruched detailing on the curtains, and *Complement* large cord on tape as trimming on the upholstered chair. The undercurtains are of *Osterly Lace.*

RIGHT

Nancy Loney of New York and Rhode Island designed this bedroom with its evocative, vintage painted furniture using *Sycamore* plaid for curtains and furniture.

Brunschwig & Fils®

◄ Westchester Showroom

Corporate Offices ▶

What's New?
Company Business

Since its founding in France more than one hundred years ago, Brunschwig & Fils has been a family business. The corporate headquarters is now in North White Plains, New York, but the sophisticated taste of French style is still respected. French-born Colonel Brunschwig (the *Fils* in the firm's name) married American-born Francophile decorator Zelina Comegys—thereafter known as Mrs. B. Her sisters, Celeste and Cornelia, were the mothers of both Chairman Thomas Peardon and Vice Chairman Murray Douglas.

Having no children themselves, Colonel Brunschwig and Mrs. B. nurtured and trained their niece and nephew to be part of the company. Murray, the older of the two, showed unmistakable talent as an art student and apprenticed in the design studio, eventually becoming vice president of design and then vice president and spokesperson for the company. She is now vice chairman and coauthor of this book as well as its predecessor, *Brunschwig & Fils Style*. An adept watercolorist, lecturer, and tireless worker on preservation and design committees, Murray also teaches at the New York School of Interior Design. In 2001 she was given the Royal Oak Timeless Design Award, and in 2003 she was selected by *House Beautiful* to receive the prestigious title Giant of Design.

Her cousin Tom Peardon used his business acumen and became president of Brunschwig & Fils and is now chairman, a position he likes "because it relieves me from daily nitty-gritty decisions and gives me a broader overall view of the company's direction. In the last ten years, huge effort has been poured into the computer systems, giving out much-needed information. No one realizes how detailed these are,

OPPOSITE

The entrance to the Brunschwig & Fils corporate offices at North White Plains, New York, were revamped to include a new and busy ground-floor designer's showroom, to the left, and stairs to the executive offices, to the right.

This snapshot, taken at a Brunschwig & Fils annual sales meeting, shows Chairman Thomas Peardon and Olivier, his son, who is currently responsible for information systems worldwide, enjoying each other's company.

with complications such as designers' reserves, their cuttings for approval, and so on. If you don't give great service, you can have the most beautiful products in the world, but. . . ." His voice peters out, the implication clear. Then finally, "I would like to see more appreciation of the grunt work, sales, the day-to-day ins and outs of accounting acclaimed."

Despite complex computer and business advances (and designers *do* acknowledge their efficient delivery), the company still makes sure it keeps the all-important human touch. As Tom Peardon points out: "We also have a nationwide call center which opens at eight in the morning and shuts at eight at night (Eastern Standard Time), answering to an eight hundred number. The early ones may be answering calls from showrooms in Europe and at eight at night taking calls from the West Coast. But many clients now order after working hours from the comfort of their homes."

The company also maintains its French beginnings despite its American headquarters. Tom Peardon's wife, Eveline, is French and has an innate sense of design. (Their house in Bayeux, Normandy, can be seen on pp. 110-112.) His executive assistant, Joëlle Tessier, is French and imparts a Gallic air to the North White Plains offices. Tom Peardon's son, Olivier, was educated in Europe and America and served in the French navy and still maintains an apartment in Paris (see it on pp. 113-115).

Olivier came to the North White Plains headquarters after three years of working for Brunschwig & Fils in Paris. He was responsible for all aspects of the opening of the showroom in rue du Mail. "He opened it to the trade, and proceeded to sell. It has prospered," says Tom Peardon, his proud father. Brunschwig & Fils is now highly respected as a major competitor in the French market.

The company's motto, "Good Design Is Forever," was coined by Zelina Brunschwig, its implication being that the classic documentary prints she collected will always be favorites in some form. As the company has grown, a new slogan, "Wherever You Look, the Look Is Brunschwig," reflects the company's growing diversification. The slogan has been translated into French as *"Le Style Brunschwig, un Art de Vivre."* Chairman Peardon points out that while Mrs.

The new Westchester showroom, fitted into the ground floor of the corporate offices in North White Plains, New York, is managed by Joan Drummond, who previously had worked in the Brunschwig sales office and is popular with designers from Westchester, Connecticut, and New Jersey.

President of Brunschwig & Fils Patrick Mongiello seen in his office in North White Plains, New York.

Brunschwig set the standards of design and philosophy for the company, one must understand that in the more than twenty years since her death, the company has evolved far beyond where it was then. Upholstered furniture, lighting, tables, and mirrors have been added, in addition to vast changes taking place in design and marketing— all without losing the fundamental principles.

The business seems likely to continue in the family. Olivier is now at the corporate headquarters handling future strategies of Brunschwig's complex worldwide computer system. He and his wife, Susannah, have just had a baby girl, Allegra, so the world may yet see the company called Brunschwig & *Fille!*

The new president, Patrick Mongiello, is a longtime member of the extended Brunschwig family by virtue of having worked in almost every area of the business, from sample room to product development. "We've always had a collaborative, family atmosphere here. Consultants came by recently to analyze our systems and found us unlike other companies this size. Almost every day a group of us meets and talks about all the issues in the company," Patrick says.

Traditional fabrics, especially prints, were still a major part of the business in the early 1990s. In the Color Association of the United States (CAUS) bulletin, Murray Douglas was quoted as saying, "During the 1990s, home design went through a colorless period and the trend was to all white or beige rooms, a sort of 'modernizing' period. It seems that the traditionalists are restating their attachment to color, more formal fabrics and setting their cherished collections back in the spotlight." Nevertheless, wovens (as compared with prints) now comprise just over half of textile sales, a figure— and change of image—that may surprise many customers. The sale of woven fabrics has surpassed prints due to a change in the design mood and because of this, Tom Peardon notes, "we have expanded our woven collections." These include solid, textured, and figured fabrics, in addition to plaids, checks, and stripes, which have in many cases become the pattern in a room.

The company is also far more international, not only in sales, but in offering products from abroad. Pat Mongiello brought in whole new collections from France (Verel de Belval), Spain (Gaston y Daniela), Italy (Decortex), and Thailand (Jagtar). Says Pat, "These different-looking fabrics marry into our collection very well."

Further, the furniture collection he initiated in 1986 (started with three upholstered pieces) has expanded so enormously that a new warehouse has been added to the football-field-length warehouse that already adjoins the corporate offices rotunda in North White Plains.

International

Brunschwig & Fils now has a total of twenty-six showrooms worldwide. Two are in Australia, "a rapidly growing market," says Pat Mongiello, "and the most similar to American style." Other showrooms—such as the large one in New York, which incorporates the Studio and Archive—were expanded and refurbished in the late 1990s. A new showroom serving Westchester county, New York, as well as parts of Connecticut and New Jersey, has been merged into the ground floor of the corporate rotunda in North White Plains. "Clients are delighted," says Tom Peardon, "because there is none of the New York traffic hassle—here, there is always free parking space!"

One of two new Australian showrooms, the one in Melbourne features an ensemble of the latest fabrics, furniture, lamps, tables, and wallpaper.

TOP
A long shot of the Brunschwig showroom in Paris.

CENTER
The new Los Angeles showroom reflects the West Coast style with its ample size; half-covered, skylighted, curved roof; and palm trees.

BOTTOM
This room-setting vignette at the Brunschwig & Fils exhibition at the Musée de l'Impression sur Étoffes in Mulhouse, Alsace, features *Herbier de Mr. Peter* (a document design from the Musée des Arts Décoratifs), *Ananas Exotique* cotton print (a document design from the Cooper-Hewitt Museum), *Coraux* on the cushion, and a *Sherwood* love seat. The furniture also includes a *Sherwood* chair and ottoman.

Special Orders Asked about his new title as director of North American sales, Tom Marshall says, "It doesn't feel any different." He is still involved with the Contract, Hospitality, and Special Order departments. "I have a very good staff, which is key. And I rely on the regional managers and showroom managers to keep me informed."

Christian Cordes, a member of Tom Marshall's staff, is heavily involved with special orders—and the foot soldier for a lot of the reproduction and restoration work that we do. Cordes works closely with Virginia Ruppert on Special Products, which is still handled through Tom Marshall's department. Special Order includes the growing Hospitality and Contract business (see pp. 134–151). It might also entail producing a minimum fifty-yard piece of a special coloring of a print if it was originally hand screen printed. This is always marked on the selvedge. A case came up with an order for a client of designer William Kulp in New York who needed an unusual watery purple ground for the popular chintz design *Coligny.* This design, a favorite of Mrs. B's (who had used it in her Paris apartment), is a European arborescent motif based on the tree-of-life idea, but with realistic rather than fantastic Indian flowers. *Coligny*—like "Good Design"—is forever, as can be seen in the photograph of a set of comfortable, overstuffed furniture in the New York showroom covered with a pretty pale coloring of the same design. If the words "hand print" do not appear on the selvedge, it means a fabric was printed by a machine-screen process, and the minimum yardage would be greater.

TOP

Despite the full-time job of director of North American sales, Tom Marshall still loves to get involved with special projects, especially if they entail historic houses such as the White House (see pp. 64–67) and the Walt Whitman House (see pp. 46–47).

ABOVE

Working along with Tom Marshall, Christian Cordes and Virginia Ruppert supply the backbone of the Special Order Department.

Special orders can be negotiated from overseas. Head of the London showroom at Chelsea Harbour, Alan Purchase, offered this example. When London designer Michael Priest was in Barbados, he visited many of the great houses designed and decorated by the late Oliver Messel, the London theater designer, admiring his dreamy neoclassic pavilions by the sea, especially evident in Messel's own house. More recently Michael visited Flaxby Abbey, a romantic mansion in Gloucestershire with origins dating from a twelfth-century Cistercian monastery. Its owners had commissioned Messel to decorate the house, and he chose a block-printed linen that had been based on ancient crewel embroidery in a state of romantic disintegration for bed hangings in the Jacobean wing. Because Michael had admired the room so, Oliver Messel gave him a piece of the linen print.

When Michael Priest was asked to decorate a room at the June 2001 House & Garden Olympia Design Fair, he remembered Messel's Barbados house and the block-printed linen fragment in his possession and determined to use it as the inspiration for his "Caribbean Fantasy" setting. Knowing that Brunschwig often reproduced historic designs for museums, he approached the London office with Messel's document and, through the Special Products division, developed a reproduction screen print on linen that was named *Elena.* "Caribbean Fantasy" created a sensation at the fair. The printed fabric showed its versatility and worked as well as a wonderfully bleached-out seaside design as it had for a Jacobean bedroom. Michael Priest kindly sent us his watercolor illustration of the setting.

The minimum for special coloring for trimming is only fifteen yards, and the Special Order Department fills a lot of trimming orders. For special colors on woven goods, the minimum is from one hundred to two hundred yards. If it is handwoven, the minimum is much smaller, but the price goes way up!

Wallpapers require a fifteen-roll minimum for special colors. Sometimes certain patterns that have been discontinued are special ordered by enough different decorators to have the design reinstated in the collection. This happened with an endearingly comical wallpaper called *Frog Treillage,* which kept cropping up as a special order, until it was finally included in the spring 2004 collection, created specially for children's rooms.

Special Products includes the more complex and costly business of reproducing from scratch a documentary design for a historic house or museum or for someone who has just bought a private period house and has located a wallpaper that was in it and wants to reproduce it, as in the case of a wallpaper found at a house called Talavera in Claverack, New York. *Talavera* was put into Brunschwig's line of wallpapers in the early 1990s. "*Talavera* still goes on and had a new incarnation in fall 2003," says Tom Marshall. "Let's see; it's been a wallpaper, a cotton-and-linen print, a warp silk print, and is now being introduced as a silk woven design, scaled down considerably."

This print, called *Elena,* was created by Special Order on linen for London designer Michael Priest. It is based on a design given to him by the well-known set designer and decorator Oliver Messel, who had used it in a bedroom at Flaxby Abbey, Gloucestershire.

BELOW

This watercolor painted by London decorator Michael Priest is of his "Caribbean Fantasy" setting at the 2001 House & Garden Olympia Design Fair, where he used *Elena.*

Furnishings As the size and number of Brunschwig & Fils showrooms increased in the 1990s, more space opened up for display—settings incorporating all product categories. In addition to showcasing merchandise, these areas were designed to be pleasant places for customers to sit, meet with their clients, and work on projects. To augment the existing upholstery offerings, a collection of lamps, tables, and mirrors was introduced in 1992, with Lewis Paul in charge of its design. "The lamp and table collections are small relative to our fabric collection; consequently, I have to take great care with my selections of designs," he says. "I try to create pieces that are unique and have some special quality that makes them individual. I look all over the world for ideas and techniques to incorporate into new designs . . . the goal being to make something new rather than exactly reproduce something old." The pieces he designs can be expensive—sometimes thousands of dollars—so they are never made in huge quantities. Among the most popular pieces in the collection from its inauguration are the *Portuguese* tea table, a low red-

ABOVE

In charge of the hard-frame furnishings such as tables and chairs, as well as accessories such as lamps, Lewis Paul has to come up continually with unusual ideas.

BELOW

Brunschwig's collection of eggshell lacquer lamp bases made in Vietnam shows a distinctive contemporary take on Art Deco forms.

and-gold lacquer table with distinctive scalloped edges and an antiqued finish; the *Broughton* table; and the *Francis* wall lamp. Lewis Paul is also involved with furnishing Brunschwig & Fils showrooms, so he becomes aware of voids to be filled—a certain size of table that is needed or a missing variety of lamp. His products usually have a traditional look that blends well with the showroom settings. "I take inspiration from many things, but I usually have to avoid the strong architectural steel-and-glass looks of Gropius and Mies; our look tends to be more traditional. Some of the lamps and tables are produced in China and India. Sometimes the samples that come back bear no relationship to what I sent. A skilled Chinese artisan once added chrysanthemums onto a Georgian mirror frame even though he had a drawing to copy—he just couldn't resist adding his own personal stamp." In 2003 Lewis Paul put together an exciting collection of Art Deco–inspired lamps in beautiful black lacquer and ivory eggshell made in Vietnam using traditional time-consuming, handmade methods of the past. Now he's looking into that country's hand-carved work in soapstone. (While she was in Vietnam, Chippy Irvine watched the painstaking lacquer and carving processes being

done.) None of the hard-furnishing items is sold as an antique—though it is entirely possible this is how future generations may perceive them.

Brunschwig's design studio is located in Manhattan. The vice president of design, Albert Sardelli, works with a staff of that includes artists, print and woven colorists, scheme organizers, an executive assistant, an archivist, and production people. Albert knows that Brunschwig & Fils products require a classic, timeless look: "Ours is not a disposable business. Quality is our stock in trade."

Albert sees that a growing number of people are turning to decorators for help with their houses and apartments: "It is no longer the luxury it was, available to the rich only. Along with this growing number of decorators of all calibers and their clients, this creates a whole new world. Most of those new to it are nervous of making too bold a statement—they want to play safe—and wovens are safe! These new customers have not been raised in the traditional wealthy group who know and love the great printed designs such as *Le Lac, Verrières, La Portuguaise,* and *Fabriano.*"

Wovens
Wovens are considered less "formal," though there was a time when chintz—used so refreshingly and successfully by Elsie de Wolfe—was "less formal" than heavy velvet, brocade, and silk damask. Woven textures are relaxed and nonthreatening for most people, and they go with our increasingly casual lifestyle. "There is a perceived value in wovens," says Albert Sardelli; "they are weighty, while print costs are high. Our customers have accepted synthetics more in wovens than in prints. We print mostly on linen (which takes color well, and its casual, rough texture goes with our lifestyle) but also on cotton and linen, cotton, glazed cotton (chintz), silk, and synthetics in the growing Contract or Hospitality areas, where cleaning, washability, and hard-wearing qualities count more than aesthetic effect." He continues: "Customers who cannot tell the difference between a polyester taffeta or silk tend to prefer the synthetic because it is easy to wash." Synthetics such as Trevira are being used increasingly in the growing Hospitality part of the business because they can be flameproofed and still retain a luxuriant hand. But nothing takes color like silk because of its natural reflective qualities.

Aiding Albert with the woven fabrics is Talin Zerdelian, who works with various (mostly European) mills. As she describes it, "Textured wovens have depth—such as a chenille. Figured wovens have a specific scattered or prominent motif. The fabrics themselves suggest their use, and this influences their color range. We may have as many as twenty colorways if a fabric looks useful in many rooms. But the wovens have to be interesting—not something you can find just anywhere."

Outdoor Living Collection
A new technical breakthrough in 2004 was Brunschwig's fabric developed from the automotive industry for car covers, awnings, beach umbrellas—things for outdoor use that did not need to be soft to the touch. The new fabric is still made of 100 percent acrylic and is lightfast and mildew resistant but has all these qualities built into the yarn itself before it is woven. Solid colors can be solution dyed—that is, dyed before the thread is extruded for weaving, and even more innovative, it can be printed with a design. An Outdoor Living collection of excellent summer

prints, wovens, and trimmings has been assembled. This collection will go a long way toward solving the problem of colors fading in bright sunlight.

Children's Collection
In the spring of 2004, Brunschwig & Fils introduced for the first time a complete, integrated collection of fabrics and wallpapers designed specifically for children's rooms. The two theme prints *Strike up the Band* (in four colorways) and *Wild Thing* (in five colorways) were backed up by a ticking-style stripe called *Streamers* (in nine colorways), *Bravo,* a confetti-dotted print, and a cheerful multicolor *Party Plaid. Streamers* is also a wallpaper, with *Strike up the Band* and *Wild Thing* also available as wallpaper borders.

ABOVE

Brunschwig's new Outdoor Living collection gives lightfast and mildew-resistant qualities to an array of summer fabrics. The fabric is pleasant to the hand (unlike harsh awning canvas) and can be used for outdoor cushions, seating, and even umbrellas for sun or rain.

RIGHT

Against a background of *Bravo* multicolored dots is the wallpaper border of *Walk on the Wild Side*—based on a documentary design—and the shopping bag with *Strike Up the Band* border. The bag has the nice touch of being lined with *Bravo* dots.

Jagtar Silk Collection   In 2003 the new Jagtar Thai silk collection was introduced. The silk cloth comes in many different weights and can be used for upholstery. If a lighter weight is desired to match lighter-weight curtains, an adhesive backing can be used. Because these silks are woven on commercial looms, they are very well priced.

Pile Fabrics   Another popular fabric is chenille; it is less expensive to produce than velvet, and many people prefer its more casual look. The yarn is made like a pipe cleaner (it is named after a caterpillar), whereas velvet is woven like a sandwich and then sliced through the "filling" to produce a pile effect on each inner side. Single velvets, such as the famous *Tiger* and *Leopard* ones, are far more expensive because they have to be hand cut while they are slowly being woven.

Advertising and Public Relations   Also in the New York offices are those who prepare the spring and fall presentations of fabric collections. Director of Advertising and Public Relations Robert Raymond, and his assistant Stephen Dahlquist, work with an outside advertising company, and all are aided in background research by archivist Judy Straeten. They create a presentation brochure, using photographs of room settings, for each collection. Once the fabrics (in the form of swatches), wallpapers, and trimmings are available, an outside designer, freelancer Bill Walter, works with the Brunschwig team to find a suitable location for photography. He draws rough sketches of the various rooms suggesting wallpaper; backgrounds; paint coloring; floor covering; curtains; new products such as lamps, tables, and accessories; and pieces of upholstered Brunschwig furniture to best display the new fabrics. The photography itself may take as long as a week.

Scheming   Each new fabric is labeled and marked "new," and each print is "schemed," that is, given an attached set of coordinating swatches or trimmings to suggest possibilities and save busy designers time. In charge of

selecting these is David Drozdis. The new collections are presented at sales meetings, and brochures are sent to showrooms and customers.

One of the finishing touches for a collection is a new shopping bag. We all know the famous Brunschwig gray-black-and-white bag with red lettering, but new bags, with contrast linings, are always eye-catching.

ABOVE

David Drozdis, in the scheme room, decides which are the best coordinating fabrics for new prints.

RIGHT TOP

Bill Walter's sketch, and a brochure photograph show a *Directoire fauteuil* upholstered in *Balthazar* silk velvet stripe. Swatches include *Nail Head* matt gimp, *Zanzibar* silk herringbone, *Piazzetta* woven texture, and *Alberti* linen damask.

RIGHT CENTER

Swatches from the spring 2003 collection show *Lady's Slipper* lampas, which, though woven, resembles an embroidered orchid. Bill Walter's preliminary sketch and the final brochure photograph are also pinned to the wall.

RIGHT BOTTOM

This group of swatches shows *Eden* embroidery, a design based on an eighteenth-century document. A bold shot of yellow and blue-and-white stripes edge the bed hangings in the brochure photograph. Other fabrics in this collection are *Pétassoun* matelassé and *Mignonette* pinpoint stripe. The sketch is by Bill Walter.

Glossary
Decorating Terms

In the rarified world of haute décor, French, English (as well as American), and Italian words are often used. Here is a list of useful decorating and technical terms that might help the reader.

ALL-OVER: Refers to a printed fabric or wallpaper that is fairly densely covered with a small, repeating pattern.

ANTIQUE VELVET: Unless it is *really* old, this is a velvet that has been made to look distressed and older than it is.

ARABESQUE: An Arab-inspired sinuous design. Arabesques developed into delicate, interlaced patterns of curlicues and traceries incorporating acanthus leaves, classical figures, urns, medallions and/or grotesques based on Roman murals, paintings, and stucco reliefs. (Roman art was popularized in the eighteenth century by the "grand tours" of young British gentlemen, by the discovery of Pompeii, and by the Adam brothers.) Arabesques were typical of many late-eighteenth- and early-nineteenth-century designs.

ARISTOLOCHES: Seventeenth-century scroll patterns.

AUBUSSON: Handwoven carpet or tapestry with a distinctive style, named after the town in France where the style originated. Since the carpets are made with a tapestry weave, they are typically flat.

BALDACHIN: A high, draped, crown-shaped structure over a bed, dais, or throne (from the Italian *baldacchino*).

BANYAN: Indian name for a man's at-home robe or dressing gown, from the eighteenth century.

BATIK: A patterned fabric produced by coating areas not to be dyed with wax. Originally from Indonesia.

BENGALINE: A lustrous fabric with ribs made from heavy cords in the filling.

BERGÈRE: A large, deep armchair with closed arms and a seat cushion.

BLOCK FRINGE: Usually a straight-cut fringe in blocks of color. (It is sometimes seen with a more delicate, fan-shaped edge.)

BLOCK PRINTING: Hand printing using wood blocks onto which a design has been carved. The blocks are coated from a dye pad and applied to cloth. (Somewhat similar to linoleum or potato printing done in schools.)

BLOTCH PRINT: A printing effect whereby the ground area (which can be quite large) is colored in addition to the patterned area.

BOISERIE: Decorative wood carving, especially paneling.

BORDER (ON WALLPAPER): Printed wallpaper edges from one inch wide to as much as a foot wide. These often have to be hand trimmed before applying.

BROCADING: A complex form of weaving to create an embroidered effect. Usually silk or metal threads are wrapped around the warp threads to form raised designs. (See *lampas* for comparison.)

BROCATELLE: A sculptured, low-relief Jacquard pattern in a satin weave. A brocatelle is backed for strength by extra-filling yarns of cotton or linen, which do not appear on the surface but give a raised effect.

CALENDERING: The effect of a sheen produced by a calender machine, which consists of a set of heavy rollers mounted on vertical frames. The cloth is passed between the rollers. By the differing use of heat, pressure, surface friction, and variety of rollers, possible finishes include chasing, glazing, watermarking, and *moirage*. A calendered finish is usually softer than a more-brilliant glazed finish (see *glazed*).

CANAPÉ: A small sofa (when not an hors d'oeuvre!) introduced under Louis XIV, usually en suite with armchairs—bergères or *fauteuils.*

CARTOUCHE: A decorative arrangement of attributes, such as musical instruments or gardening tools. (See *Tanguy's Trophies,* p. 104, for an example on printed cloth and p. 107 for Rosemary Burgher's cartouche of real garden implements.)

CHAÎNE: A French word meaning the warp on a loom.

CHENILLE: A fabric made using chenille yarn, which is fuzzy like a caterpillar (from the French word for "caterpillar").

CHINÉ: Literally, "made Chinese," but the term came to be used by the French for anything exotic, especially warp-dyed fabrics.

CHINTZ: Printed cotton fabric used mostly in interior decoration; it often has a glazed finish (from an Indian word).

CHOU: A crumpled puff of fabric used to accent curtain swags or used at the top and/or bottom of chandelier-chain covers or on overhead bed drapery (from the French for "cabbage").

CISELÉ VELVET: A combination of cut and uncut velvet (from the French for "sculptured" or "chiseled").

COMPOUND WEAVES: Fabrics with more than one warp and more than one filling (or weft). Some, such as a brocaded ottoman or a combination of damask and brocading, can be so complex they require a month just to set up the loom. (And skilled French craftsmen cannot be rushed—if they fall ill you have to wait until they get better!) The fabric in Mme de Pompadour's bedchamber on pp. 44–45 is a compound weave lampas.

CONVERTER: The person or business responsible for converting greige goods into finished, printed fabric.

COPPER-PLATE PRINTING: A printing process using engraved or etched copper plates. Copper plating on fabric and on china was a development from the paper-printing profession.

CORDING: Twisted or braided cord in a number of sizes and variations, either applied or inserted into upholstery, cushion, or pillow edges to add color and definition. When cording becomes more than an inch in diameter, it is often referred to as rope. Cords are often sold as "cord on tape," for easier insertion.

CORDUROY: Any one of many variations of velvety-pile fabrics cut into vertical ribs or wales. Uncut corduroy has a ribless pile (from the French *corde du roi*—originally it was a regal fabric).

COUP DE SABRE: A time-consuming process whereby certain surface threads of heavy satin (usually printed) are cut by hand with a sharp knife to raise threads in order to form a pile texture on specific parts of a design.

CREWEL: Designs based on a particular type of late-seventeenth-century English embroidery using wool on unbleached linen. The patterns usually combine leaves, vines, flowers, and animals.

DADO: The lower part of an interior wall, usually (but not necessarily) below the chair rail, especially when the lower portion is decorated or made of a different material from the upper wall.

DAMASK: A fabric named after the Syrian city of Damascus, created by combining two weaves, twill and satin. Damask is reversible (satin weave on one side, twill weave on the other) and limited to two colors: warp and weft threads.

DÉCOUPAGE: A design formed from cutout and rearranged pieces of a material, usually paper.

DIMITY: A heavy, everyday cloth in the eighteenth century; a medium-weight fabric in the nineteenth century; a lightweight, unpretentious fabric today. Dimity usually has a patterned weave, most often with vertical ribs. (See *New Richmond* dimity at George Washington's house Mount Vernon on p. 63.)

DIRECTOIRE: A style in France during the early years of Bonaparte's power (1795–99), before Napoléon became emperor.

DISTRICT CHECK: A houndstooth check with a larger, contrasting check dividing it (named by Scottish tweed makers).

DOBBY: A weave requiring special loom adjustments to produce small, symmetrical, repeating motifs. Fabrics made of this weave are sometimes described as "figured woven." Named for the English "dobby boy," who sat atop the loom and lifted the warp threads (from "dobbin," a term for a workhorse).

DOCUMENTARY: In fabric or wallpaper terms, this is a print based on a proven historic design.

DUPION: Strong slubbed silk formed from double cocoons called dupions.

DYE LOTS: Batches of printed or dyed fabric. Sometimes colors vary slightly from one dye lot to another. (See *run number.*)

EGGSHELL LACQUER: A fine, many-layered lacquer that uses real eggshells to form a crackled effect.

EMBOSSING: A design pressed into fabric with heat, rather like making a waffle. (See *gaufrage.*)

EMPIRE: Pronounced "Om-peer." A style in France when Napoléon was emperor (1804–15), roughly around the time of the Regency in England and the Federal period in the United States. Design motifs include bees, Roman details, stripes, tents, and the neoclassic look. There is also the Second Empire style, which is florid in comparison, from when—as far as style was concerned—Empress Eugénie and her couturier, Worth, ruled Paris (1852–70).

ENFILADE: A series of rooms—or other objects—leading from one to the next in a straight line. Decorators love this word; a less fancy word for the same thing is "shotgun."

EN SUITE: A decorating scheme that uses the same fabric on walls, curtains, upholstery, bed hangings, and bed covers.

FALL-ON: A term used to describe one color overprinting another, as in yellow printed on blue to produce green.

FAN EDGING: Loop-fringed trimming inserted or applied to a fabric, giving a distinctive, wavy effect; it can be colored in blocks.

FAUTEUIL: A French word for an armchair.

FAUX: Painted effects that simulate real materials (from the French for "false").

FELT: A fabric formed by matting fibers—usually wool—under heat and pressure.

FIGURED VELVET: A patterned velvet with a design formed by cut and uncut loops.

FIGURED WOVEN: A weave requiring special loom adjustments to produce small, symmetrical, repeating motifs—similar to a dobby weave.

FLATBED PRINTING: A mechanized method of printing wherein the fabric moves on a bed, while the printing screens remain stationary.

FLOCKING: Short or pulverized fiber used to form a pattern when applied to cloth or paper.

FRENCH CORNERS: Gathering or pleating at the corners of cushions to give a soft, rounded effect. Furniture makers use the term "butterfly" corners, and they are sometimes called Turkish corners.

FRISÉ: A firm fabric with a pile of uncut loops (from the French word meaning "curled"); also called frieze.

FUGITIVE: A dye or color that runs when washed or fades quickly in sunlight.

GAMME: Colored squares outside the trim line of wallpaper and on the selvedge of printed fabric that show the number of colors used (from the French for "scale" or "gamut").

GAUFRAGE: A process whereby fabric is embossed with a heated weight to create a pattern (from the Flemish for "waffle").

GIMP: A flat, narrow (usually between three eighths to one half inch wide) woven trimming that comes in a variety of raised patterns; often used on wood-frame furniture to cover upholstery tacks, but also used in many decorative ways on walls, edges of lamp shades, and pillows.

GISELLES: A French term for supple silk fringes that create a soft zigzag effect; often called fan-edge fringe.

GLAZED: A term to describe a glossy fabric surface, produced by heat, heavy-pressure chemical action, or a glazing substance. It is a finish that goes in and out of fashion, but it is a practical finish because it is so dust-resisting.

GOBELINS: The name of a French state tapestry firm in Paris, founded under Henri IV and still going.

GOBLET PLEAT: A version of a pinched curtain pleat with the upper part stiffened with buckram or puffed out in some way to suggest a goblet.

GRAIN: The true warp or direction of vertical threads of a fabric. This can be established by running the point of a pin down the cloth or by measuring in from the selvedge.

GREIGE GOODS: Pronounced "gray." Plain, unfinished goods for printing.

GRISAILLE: A pattern in tones of gray or sepia sometimes used on wallpaper to give the illusion of sculpture.

GROSGRAIN: A ribbed fabric; also a ribbed ribbon.

GROS POINT: A needlework effect worked by hand with a blunt needle on an open-spaced canvas. It can be imitated as fabric.

GROTESQUES: From the word "grotto," decorative patterns not unlike arabesque curlicues, using Italian Baroque–inspired details such as human figures, animal forms, and masks.

GROUND: The field or background of a pattern.

HAND BLOCK: See *block printing*. ("Hand blocking" can also refer—in a completely different way—to hat blocking, needlepoint blocking, and the hand blocking of knitted items.)

HAND PRINT: Originally this meant a design manually printed by flat screens, but the term now includes simulated hand-screen printing, which allows for drying time between each color (printing "wet on dry").

HEAD COLORS: The colors in a printed design that form the pattern. The background color is called the blotch.

HEALTH CARE: A trade term for the interior design of hospitals and health-care offices.

HEDDLES: A device on a loom, worked by a foot pedal, that lifts the warp yarns so the shuttle can be passed through.

HERRINGBONE: A weave in which twills, or diagonal weaves, alternate directions, forming a zigzag pattern.

HORSEHAIR: A cloth used extensively for upholstery in the eighteenth and nineteenth centuries, with a weft made from hair from horses' tails. Real horsehair fabric is only about twenty-one inches wide. (See pp. 196–197 for examples *Metamorphosis* and *Ruffle Your Feathers,* which are embroidered horsehair.) Real horsehair is in the natural colors of the horse and comes plain and in simple-figured weaves. Good synthetic horsehair fabrics are available in standard widths.

HOSPITALITY: A trade term for interior design of restaurants, inns, hotels, and other spaces where the public is housed or entertained.

IKAT: Warp-dyed fabrics, originally from Indonesia, India, and Afghanistan. The warp is printed or tie-dyed before weaving.

IMBERLINE: A type of fabric with a woven striped ground and a large damask pattern used since the eighteenth century for upholstery and wall hangings.

INDIENNE: Fabric inspired by India. The first colorful and colorfast painted or penned cottons were from India. (See *kalamkari.*)

INTERLINING: Material inserted between the face and lining of curtains, coverlets, or table skirts to provide body or insulation and/or to prevent light from shining through.

JABOT: In curtain making, vertical folds of fabric draped to reveal contrasting undersides, intended to soften and embellish a window more than to be drawn to block light.

JACQUARD WEAVING: Method of weaving large patterned designs using punched cards, named after the Frenchman Joseph-Marie Jacquard (1752–1834). Weavers, fearing for their jobs, burned his invention when it was first fitted to Lyon's looms, in 1812. Eventually they accepted it as better, faster, and a good thing for all. Jacquard fabrics are those woven on a Jacquard loom.

JASMIN: A French passementerie term for a chain of tiny, silk-covered loops and flowerlike shapes.

JASPÉ: A word used by some English textile makers to describe an effect similar to *strié*—a fine, uneven, textured, vertical-stripe pattern. *Strié* was originally made by dripping dye down paper or fabric.

KALAMKARI: Literally, "pen work." The term describes colorful, originally hand-decorated, cotton textiles produced in India. (See p. 7.)

KNIFE EDGE: A term used to describe seat pads and cushions (pillows) with no insert of fabric to add thickness to the shape.

KNOCKOFF: A slang term for an unauthorized copy of a pattern or style (usually a cheaper version).

LACE: Open-work fabric or edging often made from thread or cut and embroidered. The many variations of lace include Alençon lace, Chantilly lace, Cluny lace, guipure lace, Nottingham lace, Scottish lace, Val lace, Venise lace, tatting, and more.

LAMÉ: A fabric made using metallic thread or synthetic metallic thread.

LAMPAS: A compound woven cloth with figured patterns, bulkier than a true brocaded cloth because all the additional wefts needed for the design are woven into the back of the fabric and carried from selvedge to selvedge. (See *compound weaves*.)

LATTICE: A framework of crossed strips of wood or metal or a decorative imitation of this.

LEADING EDGES: The edges of a curtain—often trimmed in some way—that meet when a curtain is closed.

LOCK STITCH: A machine stitch that is often used to outline fabric designs on quilts. Unlike a chain stitch, a lock stitch will not pull out in one thread if it catches on jewelry or a cat's claw.

LOOSEBACK: Refers to soft, upholstered furniture with separately made seat-back cushions. (Tightback furniture has cushioning built into the back.)

LOZENGE: A decorative, elongated diamond shape used often in carpet and fabric designs.

MACHINE PRINT: Patterns printed by mechanical means rather than by hand.

MADDER: A natural dye made from a plant, formerly used to create colors ranging from aubergine to pink.

MATELASSÉ: A double-woven textile with a quilted appearance.

MÉDAILLON: A circular or oval shape used decoratively to frame a motif or vignette. Especially popular on fabric during Napoléon's Empire period.

MEZZARO: Italian term for a large printed square or rectangular shawl worn by women in Genoa, a center of fabric printing since the eighteenth century. *Mezzari* were often based on Indian tree-of-life designs but usually were horizontal because of the way they were worn rather than vertical like palampores.

MOIRÉ: Fabric with a watered-silk appearance. Originally produced by applying huge pressure from heated cylinders. Now available in woven or printed versions. The French term is *moire*. The process is called *moirage*.

MORDANT: A chemical that fixes dyes, making printed cloth washable and the dye colorfast.

MOREEN: A plain weave, usually wool with a weft heavier than the warp, which gives a ribbed effect. Can be moiréd or embossed to simulate damask. Used mainly in historic houses.

MOSS FRINGE: A silky, cut-edged, fringed braid, usually inserted. It often looks most effective when the fringe is doubled and, therefore, fuller.

MULL: A fine, sheer fabric, usually cotton, but sometimes of silk.

NAIL HEADS: Large-headed metal nails, sometimes brass, sometimes with fancy designs, used to hold upholstery fabric to a wooden chair frame. A Brunschwig & Fils trimming in several colors called *Nail Head* imitates this effect.

NAP: The direction in which the pile of a fabric is brushed, especially on velvets and corduroys.

NOISETTES: A passementerie term for small, decorative, acorn shapes covered in silk threads.

OMBRÉ: A shaded effect (French for "shadowed").

ONE WAY: A printed (or woven) pattern that has one direction that is definitely up.

OTTOMAN: A fabric with a silky, ribbed effect that runs from selvedge to selvedge. Technically, the fabric requires two wefts of unequal thickness to produce ribs. An ottoman is also a large, padded footstool, often used with an upholstered armchair.

PAISLEY: A design based on the Indian cone motif, named after Paisley, Scotland, where soft wool shawls were produced in variations on these patterns, copying the more expensive originals made in Kashmir, India.

PALAMPORES: A coverlet (from the Indian word); also, a hanging typically patterned with a large tree-of-life motif such as *Karikal* (see pp. 8–11).

PASSEMENTERIE: Any type of cord, braid, fringe, tieback, or tassel used for embellishment. Can range from a simple edging to an elaborate, handmade, two-thousand-dollar confection!

PATINA: In fabric and furniture, an antiqued look, sometimes achieved through age and sometimes contrived.

PELMET: A decorative band, drape, or ruffle used to hide the pulley system on curtains. Also called a valance.

PENCILED BLUE: A process used for early indienne designs in which indigo dye was "penciled" (painted) on top of yellow to produce green.

PICOT EDGE: A tiny knot effect, often at the edge of ribbon, that gives a romantic, feminine effect.

PIECE-DYED: Fabric that is dyed after it is woven. A "piece" is a fifty-yard length of fabric. (See *yarn-dyed fabric.*)

PINCH PLEATS: Groups of pleats at the top of a curtain. Many variations exist, some formed using commercial pleating tape, others stitched individually to conform with a fabric's design.

PIPING: See *welt.*

PLATE PRINTING: A process wherein engraved plates are used to print monotone toiles. Originally the plates were flat; later, metal cylinders were employed to speed printing. Also called copper-plate printing.

PLATFORM: In furniture, the horizontal area of a chair or sofa that seat pads or cushions sit on.

PLISSÉ: A seersucker effect obtained by loom tension or by heat pressing.

PLUSH: Velvet with a very high pile.

POINT RENTRÉ: A weaving technique invented in the early eighteenth century by Jean Revel which allows colors to shade into one another for greater naturalism.

PONGEE: Usually refers to a type of unbleached, plain-weave silk.

POWER LOOM: A loom operated by mechanical means, not by hand.

PRINT ROOM: A wall-decorating conceit dating from the eighteenth century for ladies and gentlemen of leisure of pasting classical engravings directly onto a plain-colored wall and applying printed frames and connecting decorations such as lion heads, masks, cords, chains, ribbons, and garlands to produce a pleasing and somewhat erudite composition.

PUDDLE: The amount by which a curtain or table cover flows onto the floor. Can vary from one to eight inches—more than that is excessive.

RAILROADING: A method by which the goods are cut sideways down the grain, as opposed to the orthodox method of cutting across the grain and then matching the print on each seam. Railroading is useful for nondirectional fabrics to save needless seams.

RÉCAMIER: A neoclassic sofa for reclining, made fashionable by Mme Récamier, a great beauty at the time of Napoléon's empire.

RÉGENCE: A French style from the period when Philippe duc d'Orléans was regent after Louis XIV's death and before Louis XV reached his maturity (1715–23), a period of suppleness and grace in the decorative arts.

REPEAT: The length of a printed or woven pattern before it repeats itself. A large repeat is usually more expensive to use because more cloth is required to match the seams correctly.

RESIST PRINT (OR DYE): A method of creating a pattern by covering certain areas before dyeing, often with wax, which is then removed after dyeing. A series of dye baths can be used to make multicolored designs.

ROLLER PRINTING: Printing by means of an engraved revolving cylinder.

ROSETTE: A flat, circular ornament made of fabric or pleated ribbon and used as decorative punctuation.

ROTARY SCREEN PRINTING: A mechanized form of screen printing, wherein dye is forced through a cylindrical drum onto moving fabric.

ROUGE D'ANDRINOPLE: The French phrase for Turkey red—named after the Middle Eastern city.

RUN NUMBER: The number of a specific printing of a wallpaper—similar to a dye lot for fabrics.

SATEEN: A cotton fabric in a satin weave.

SATIN WEAVE: A weave in which the weft threads intersect with the warp at long intervals to produce a smooth, reflective, lustrous effect.

SCREEN ENGRAVER: The artist-craftsman who translates a design onto a screen (an important person in the art of fabric printing).

SCREEN PRINTING: In today's terms, a process in which rotary screens are used for each color. The fabric moves quickly under the screens, not allowing for drying time. Also called wet-on-wet printing.

SELF PIPING: Piping (welt) made from the same fabric as the body of a curtain, wall covering, cushion, or upholstery.

SELVEDGE: The woven edge of a piece of cloth. On a printed decorative fabric, this is where you often find the name of the company that created it, a color *gamme* indicating the number of colors, and arrows indicating the up direction of the fabric.

SHANTUNG: A form of slubbed silk, usually unbleached.

SHOT: An iridescent effect achieved by having the warp and weft of different colors, as, for instance, in taffeta or other plain weaves.

SIDEWALL: A term used for wallpaper covering the main body of the wall, as opposed to the borders and panels.

SLUB: Fibers are slubbed when they vary from thick to thin, which creates a texture in the weave.

SOCIABLE: A circular, tufted sofa popular in the nineteenth century.

SOFA À BORNE: A French term for a sociable.

SOUTACHE: A narrow braid, originally used on military uniforms, usually top-stitched onto fabric in a central groove (from the Hungarian *sujás*).

SQUAB: An English term for a removable seat pad on a chair.

STRIÉ: A fine, uneven, vertical stripe. (See also *jaspé*.)

STRIKE-OFF: A test of dye colors in print mills.

SWAG: Generally refers to a looped fold of fabric used as a valance for curtains.

TABBY: The simplest over-and-under weave, such as children use to make pot holders in kindergarten. Also called a plain weave.

TAFFETA: A plain weave made by using warp and filling yarns of equal weight, producing a firm, close fabric. We tend to think of it as a crisp, silklike fabric, but it is really a weave. Cotton taffeta is a useful decorative fabric.

TATTERSALL: A fabric once used for horse blankets, made up of lines crossed to form small squares on a plain ground. Named after a horse market in London.

TÊTE-À-TÊTE: An S-shaped divan (from the French for "head-to-head," meaning "intimate").

TIEBACKS: Devices used to hold curtains back in a graceful loop. Many different types exist, and they can be made of self fabric, metal, or passementerie (called *embrasse* in French).

TIGHTBACK: An upholstery term for armchairs and sofas without separate back upright cushions.

TOILE: A monotone print with an intricate engraved quality, often of a historic, pictorial subject. (See p. 19 for toile de Jouy.)

TON-SUR-TON: French for "tone-on-tone," such as dark beige on light beige.

TRAPUNTO: A decorative, linear, quilted design made by trapping soft cotton cords between two layers of fabric to form a raised design.

TREE OF LIFE: A classic Indian pattern of a flowering tree. The design has been adapted in many ways over the centuries.

TREILLAGE: A trellis pattern usually formed of diagonal crisscrosses. Can refer to a trellis effect on fabric or wallpaper.

TREVIRA: A polyester fiber used mainly in contract work; a registered trademark.

TRIM: A border allowance on either edge of printed wallpaper, like selvedges on fabrics, that protects the edges from damage in shipping and has to be trimmed off before the paper is hung. Also refers to passementerie.

TUFTING: A method of upholstering using buttons or decorative knots to hold in place the deep padding used in overstuffed furniture.

TURKISH CORNERS: See *French corners.*

TURK'S HEAD: A globe-shaped, decorative, handmade knot formed from cord or fabric tubing.

TUSSAH: A rough type of silk with slubs from uncultivated silkworms.

TWILL: A diagonal, stepped weave.

VALANCE: Another term for a pelmet; a heading that hides the curtain rings or pulling system.

VERMICELLI: Small, continuous, curly lines in a design (from the Italian for "worms").

VIGNETTE: A small decorative picture or ornament. In a book, often used at the beginnings or ends of chapters.

VOIDED VELVET: Jacquard-patterned cloth with areas having a velvet pile contrasting with areas without pile, giving a sculptured effect.

WARP: The threads that run down a fabric. These threads are first set up on a loom, and the weft, or filling, threads are then woven in to stabilize the cloth.

WARP PRINTING: A method of printing in which a pattern is first printed, painted, or tie-dyed on the warp threads, then a plain filler is woven in, producing a softened effect that is the same on both sides. (See *ikat.*)

WEFT: The threads that weave across the warp from selvedge to selvedge; sometimes called the filling or the woof.

WELT: Fabric cut in strips on the bias, filled with cording to form a tube, and then stitched between seams to give emphasis to slipcovers or upholstery. Also known as piping.

WOOD-BLOCK PRINTING: An early method of fabric printing produced by carving the design on a block of wood, charging it with dye, placing it on the fabric, and then tapping it to transfer the dye to the cloth. Fine and subtle effects are achieved by this method, but it requires great skill and is time consuming and, therefore, is expensive.

YARN-DYED FABRIC: Fabric made from yarn that has been dyed before being woven into cloth. Yarn-dyed fabric is superior to piece-dyed fabric because the threads are completely and individually covered in dye. In Brunschwig's Outdoor Living collection, the acrylic fiber is vat-dyed before being extruded into thread. This enables the final cloth to retain its color even in bright sunlight and makes it impervious to mildew.

Useful Listings

The lists below include historic houses and museums mentioned in the text and open to the public, Brunschwig & Fils showrooms, and independent dealers in the United States and across the world.

Historic Houses and Museums

Château de Versailles
Place d'armes
78000 Versailles
France
33 1 30 84 74 00

The main residence of the French monarchs from Louis XIV on.

Clifton House
Civic Works, 2701 St. Lo Drive
Baltimore, MD 21213
(410) 366-8533

An 1800 house set in a park. The house is now used for educational and civic events.

Cooper-Hewitt, National Design Museum, Smithsonian Institution
2 East 91st Street
New York, NY 10128
(212) 849-8400

The only museum in the United States devoted exclusively to historic and contemporary design, with a splendid wallpaper collection.

The Frick Collection
1 East 70th Street
New York, NY 10121
(212) 288-0700

Fine arts with an emphasis on the eighteenth century.

Gracie Mansion
East End Avenue at 88th Street
New York, NY 10128
(212) 570-0985

The residence of the mayor of New York.

Gunston Hall Plantation
10709 Gunston Road
Mason Neck, VA 22079
(703) 550-9220

A plantation house built by George Mason, author of the Bill of Rights.

Historic Deerfield
321 Main Street
Deerfield, MA 01342
(413) 774-5581

A collection of buildings from the Colonial period furnished with appropriate decorative arts.

The Metropolitan Museum of Art
1000 Fifth Avenue at 82nd Street
New York, NY 10028
(212) 535-7710

Mount Vernon
3200 George Washington Memorial Parkway
Mount Vernon, VA 22121
(703) 780-2000

Home of George Washington.

Mount Vernon Hotel Museum and Garden
421 East 61st Street
New York, NY 10021
(212) 838-6878

Musée des Arts Décoratifs
Palais du Louvre, 107, rue de Rivoli
75001 Paris
France
(33) 1 44 55 57 50

A great repository of furnished French rooms.

Musée de l'Impression sur Étoffes
14, rue Jean-Jacques Henner
BP 1468-68072
Mulhouse cedex
France
(33) (0)3 89 46 83 00

Guided tours and demonstrations offered.

Musée du Papier Peint du Rixheim
La Commanderie, 28, rue Zuber
BP 41
F-68171 Rixheim
France
(33) 389 64 24 56

A museum about wallpaper.

Museum of Early Southern Decorative Arts (MESDA)
924 South Main Street
Winston-Salem, NC 27101
(336) 721-7360

A collection of southern decorative arts.

The Phelps-Hatheway House
55 South Main Street
Suffield, CT 06078
(860) 247-8996

For more information, call the Antiquarian & Landmarks Society at (860) 247-8996.

Royal Ontario Museum
100 Queen's Park
Toronto, Ontario M5S 2C6
Canada
(416) 586-5549

Canada's major metropolitan museum.

The Royal Pavilion, Brighton
    Royal Pavilion Art Gallery and
    Museum
4-5 Pavilion Buildings
Brighton, East Sussex BN1 1EE
England
(44)(0) 1273 290 900

The Prince Regent's seaside extravaganza.

The Walt Whitman House
328 Nickle Boulevard
Camden, NJ 08103
(856) 964-5383

Tours by appointment; contact Leo Blake.

Westbury House and Old Westbury
    Gardens
71 Old Westbury Road
Old Westbury, NY 11568
(516) 333-0048

Garden and house open to the public on certain days.

The White House
1600 Pennsylvania Avenue NW
Washington, DC 20230
(202) 456-7041

The residence of all American presidents.

Winterthur, An American Country
    Estate
Route 52 (Kennett Pike)
Winterthur, DE 19735
(800) 448-3883

An estate and museum of decorative arts.

Brunschwig & Fils Showrooms

Businesses grow, and things change, but as we go to press these listings are up-to-date. The first list (1) indicates showrooms within the United States and Canada. The second list (2) indicates independent showroom dealers who have Brunschwig products. The third list (3) indicates the growing number of stockists throughout the world. These showrooms welcome you accompanied by your architect or decorator.

1) SHOWROOMS IN THE UNITED STATES AND CANADA

Arizona

Brunschwig & Fils
Dean-Warren Ltd.
2716 North Sixty-eighth Street
Scottsdale, AZ 85257
Tel.: (480) 947-9090
Fax: (480) 990-0595

California

Brunschwig & Fils
114 Laguna Design Center
23811 Aliso Creek Road
Laguna Niguel, CA 92677
Tel.: (949) 831-5666
Fax: (949) 831-3596

Brunschwig & Fils
2 Henry Adams Street, Suite 155
San Francisco, CA 94103
Tel.: (415) 522-1622
Fax: (415) 522-1733

Brunschwig & Fils
8687 Melrose Avenue, Suite B 653
West Hollywood, CA 90069
Tel.: (310) 659-9800
Fax: (310) 657-7174

Colorado

Brunschwig & Fils
Denver Design Center
595 South Broadway, Suite 109W
Denver, CO 80209
Tel.: (303) 733-6484
Fax: (303) 733-6485

Florida

Brunschwig & Fils
1855 Griffin Road, Suite C114
Dania Beach, FL 33004
Tel.: (954) 920-5994
Fax: (954) 920-1261

Georgia

Brunschwig & Fils
351 Peachtree Hills Avenue NE,
    Suite 125
Atlanta, GA 30305
Tel.: (404) 261-5116
Fax: (404) 233-1004

Illinois

Brunschwig & Fils
6-121 Merchandise Mart
Chicago, IL 60654
Tel.: (312) 329-0178
Fax: (312) 329-0182

Massachusetts

Brunschwig & Fils
One Design Center Place, Suite 500
Boston, MA 02210
Tel.: (617) 348-2855
Fax: (617) 348-2172

Michigan

Brunschwig & Fils
1700 Stutz Drive, Suite 28
Troy, MI 48084
Tel.: (248) 649-0505
Fax: (248) 649-0828

Minnesota

Brunschwig & Fils
D&D Associates, Inc.
275 Market Street, Suite 407
Minneapolis, MN 55405
Tel.: (612) 339-2607
Fax: (612) 339-6855

New York

Brunschwig & Fils
D&D Building
979 Third Avenue
New York, NY 10022
Tel.: (212) 838-7878
Fax: (212) 838-5611

Brunschwig & Fils
75 Virginia Road
North White Plains, NY 10603
Tel.: (914) 872-1100
Fax: (914) 872-0590

North Carolina

Brunschwig & Fils
The Foundry
619 South Cedar Street, Suite J
Charlotte, NC 28202
Tel.: (704) 375-6232
Fax: (704) 375-6342

Ohio

Brunschwig & Fils
Ohio Design Center
23533 Mercantile Road, Suite 111
Beachwood, OH 44122
Tel.: (216) 292-2650
Fax: (216) 292-3116

Pennsylvania

Brunschwig & Fils
The Marketplace
2400 Market Street, Suite 201
Philadelphia, PA 19103
Tel.: (215) 567-3730
Fax: (215) 854-0183

Texas

Brunschwig & Fils
590 Dallas Design Center
1025 North Stemmons Freeway
Dallas, TX 75207
Tel.: (214) 741-6152
Fax: (214) 742-7141

Brunschwig & Fils
5120 Woodway Drive, Suite 2016
Houston, TX 77056
Tel.: (713) 961-3391
Fax: (713) 961-0871

Washington

Brunschwig & Fils
Designers Showroom
5701 Sixth Avenue South, Suite 262
Seattle, WA 98108
Tel.: (206) 767-4454
Fax: (206) 762-6020

Washington, DC

Brunschwig & Fils
The Design Center
300 D Street SW, Suite 420
Washington, DC 20024
Tel.: (202) 554-1004
Fax: (202) 554-4393

Canada

Brunschwig & Fils
320 Davenport Road
Toronto, Ontario
M5R 1K6
Tel.: (416) 968-0699
Fax: (416) 968-6500

2) INDEPENDENT
SHOWROOM DEALERS

California

J M Design Center
1746 Junction Avenue
San Jose, CA 95112
Tel.: (408) 436-8414
Fax: (408) 436-0736

Florida

Gregory Alonso, Inc.
6210 Shirley Street, Suite 108
Naples, FL 34109
Tel.: (216) 765-1810
Fax: (216) 765-1858

Interiors Trading Co., Inc.
315 North Willow Avenue
Tampa, FL 33606
Tel.: (813) 258-6678

Interiors Trading Company of
    Orlando
1340 Gene Street
Winter Park, FL 32789
Tel.: (407) 740-4130
Fax: (407) 740-4160

Jack Walsh Trade Showroom
501 Ardmore Road
West Palm Beach, FL 33401
Tel.: (561) 659-4846
Fax: (561) 659-0968

Indiana

Albert Square, Ltd.
301 East Carmel Drive, Suite E600
Indianapolis, IN 46032
Tel.: (317) 571-1450
Fax: (317) 569-1302

Kansas

Designers Only
5225 West 75th Street
Prairie Village, KS 66208
Tel.: (913) 649-3778
Fax: (913) 722-7877

Louisiana

Delk & Morrison
320 Julia Street
New Orleans, LA 70130
Tel.: (504) 529-4939
Fax: (504) 529-4985

Ohio

DeCioccio Showroom
Longworth Hall
700 West Pete Rose Way
Cincinnati, OH 45203
Tel.: (513) 241-9573
Fax: (513) 241-9915

Style Line In
Chelsea House Fabrics
901 West Third Avenue
P.O. Box 2706
Columbus, OH 43216
Tel.: (614) 291-0600
Fax: (614) 291-0700

Pennsylvania

Gregory Alonso, Inc.
484 Lowries Run Road
Pittsburgh, PA 15237
Tel.: (412) 366-4133
Fax: (412) 366-6133

Texas

Interior Trade Cartel
18585 Sigma Road, Suite 104
San Antonio, TX 78258
Tel.: (210) 494-1602
Fax: (210) 494-1603

Stockton-Hicks & Laffey
7301 Burnett Road, Suite 200
Austin, TX 78757
Tel.: (512) 302-1116
Fax: (512) 302-1213

Virginia

Designer's Market of Richmond
2107-B North Hamilton Street
Richmond, VA 23230
Tel.: (804) 353-5224
Fax: (804) 353-5161

Canada

Annestarr Agencies
611 Alexander Street
Vancouver, British Columbia
V6A 1E1
Tel.: (604) 254-3336
Fax: (604) 254-3376

Chintz & Collections
4269 Saint Catherine Street West
Westmount, Quebec H3Z 1P7
Tel.: (514) 731-6745
Fax: (514) 731-8997

DWA Interior Furnishings Inc.
2613 Fourteenth Street SW
Calgary, Alberta
T2T 3T9
Tel.: (403) 245-4014
Fax: (403) 229-1913

3) SHOWROOMS OUTSIDE
THE UNITED STATES
AND CANADA

Australia

ADELAIDE
Greenfield Distributors
374 Fullarton Road
Fullarton SA 5063
Tel.: (61) (0) 8 8338 2229
Fax: (61) (0) 8 8339 2449

BRISBANE
In House Agencies
Level B, 36 Vernon Terrace
Teneriffe
Queensland 4005
Tel.: (61) (0) 7 3257 3499
Fax: (61) (0) 7 3257 3220

MELBOURNE
Brunschwig & Fils
751 High Street, Armadale
VIC 3143
Tel.: (61) (0) 3 9509 6766
Fax: (61) (0) 3 9509 6866

PERTH
Tessuti & Village Agency
1-2 Chelsea Village
145 Stirling Highway
Nedlands WA 6009
Tel.: (61) (0) 8 9389 8439
Fax: (61) (0) 8 9386 2696

SYDNEY
Brunschwig & Fils
88 Queen Street
Woollahra NSW 2025
Tel.: (61) (0) 2 9363 4757
Fax: (61) (0) 2 9363 2717

Austria and Germany

Hahne und Schönberg GmbH
Hessstrasse 74D-80798
Munich, Germany
Tel.: (49) 89 542 7730
Fax: (49) 89 542 77333

Belgium and Luxembourg

Bruno et Ann Porcher
Bld St. Michel 117
1040 Bruxelles, Belgium
Tel.: (32) 2 735 7576
Fax: (32) 2 735 7369

China

Mercer House Interiors Limited
19-27 Wyndham Street Central
Hong Kong
Tel.: (852) 2524 2000/1866
Fax: (852) 2524 2280

Denmark

B. Right
Hellerupvej 56
Hellerup 2900
Tel.: (45) 39 61 11 71
Fax: (45) 39 62 14 84

Egypt

(EBMTE) The Design Emporium
95 Al-Hussein Street
Dokki, P.O. 12411 Cairo
Tel.: (212) 748 3848/(212) 748 7187
Fax: (212) 761 7188

Finland

Oy Accenta Collection Ab
Merikatu 1
00140 Helsinki
Tel.: (358) 9 7771990
Fax: (358) 9 7773466

France

Brunschwig & Fils
8, rue du Mail
75002 Paris
Tel.: (33) (0) 1 44 55 02 50
Fax: (33) (0) 1 44 55 02 55

Greece

Veta Stefanidou Tsoukala
100 Kifissias Avenue
15125 Athens
Tel.: (30) 2 1 0614 1407/1412
Fax: (30) 2 10 614 2125

Indonesia

PT Internasional Quatropersisi,
Cipta Merkurius Intal.
Jl. Kemang Timur Raya # 998
Kemang Timur, Jakarta Selatan
Tel.: (62) 21 719 7308
Fax: (62) 21 719 7307

Italy

Decortex, SpA
25, via di Pagnelle
Firenze 50041 Calenzano
Tel.: (39) 055 887 3093
Fax: (39) 055 887 3096

The Netherlands

Gimko International, bv
Laan Van Meerdervoort 22
2517 AK Den Haag
Tel.: (31) 70 365 1395
Fax: (31) 70 345 9177

New Zealand

ICON Textile Ltd
Level 2, 155-165 The Strand
Parnell, Auckland
Tel.: (64) 9 302 1652
Fax: (64) 9 375 9855

Norway

Poesi Interioragentur AS
Erling Skjalgssonsgt 19 A
N-0267 Oslo
Tel.: (47) 22 12 81 80
Fax: (47) 22 12 81 90

Philippines

Elements Fine Furnishing
    Fabrics, Inc.
Ninth Floor DPC Building
2322 Pasong Tamo Extension
Makati City 1222
Tel.: (63) 2 889 8872-74
Fax: (63) 2 889 9064

Poland

Claudia Westnes Decoration
UL.Mokotowska 39
00-551 Warsaw
Tel.: (48) 22 816 1492
Fax: (48) 22 625 7722

Portugal

Pedroso y Osório, S.A.
Rua Fernão Lopes 409-2, D.T.
4150 Porto
Tel.: (351) (0) 22 616 5030
Fax: (351) (0) 22 616 5038

Russia

Decortex Ltd.
Ostojenka Str. h.10. office 225
119034, Moscow
Tel.: (7 095) 933 06 13
Fax: (7 095) 933 06 13

South Africa

Halogen International
8 Kramer Road
Kramerville, 2148
Tel.: (27) 11 448 2060
Fax: (27) 11 448 2065

Spain

Gaston y Daniela, S.A
Hermosilla 26
28001 Madrid
Tel.: (34) 91 435 2740
Fax: (34) 91 431 0358

Sweden

AB Stiltyger
Sibyllegatan 44
S-11443 Stockholm
Tel.: (46) 8 660 8630
Fax: (46) 8 661 1358

Switzerland

Agence Textile
Chemin de Rennier 2
CH-1009 Pully
Tel.: (41) 21 728 3627
Fax: (41) 21 728 3628

Taiwan

Andari Selections
6 An Ho Road, Sec 1, Lane 109
Taipei
Tel.: (886) 2 2755 0655
Fax: (886) 2 2755 4628

Turkey

E.S. Dekorasyon Tic. Ltd. Sti.
Cote Deco
Karakol Bostan Sok
    Mutlu, Apt. No. 9/2
Tesvikiye, Istanbul
Tel.: (90) 212 236 9822/3
Fax: (90) 212 2369918

United Kingdom

Brunschwig & Fils
C10 The Chambers
Chelsea Harbour Drive
London SW10 OXF, England
Tel.: (44) (o) 20 7351 5797
Fax: (44) (o) 20 7351 2280

United Arab Emirates

Brunschwig & Fils
P.O. Box 37858
Dubai
Tel.: (971) 4 339 5839
Fax: (971) 4 339 5840

One of the Brunschwig shopping bags intrigues Ruly (as in
"unruly"), the pet of one of Murray Douglas's friends.

Selected Bibliography

Books

Barber, Elizabeth Wayland. *The Mummies of Ürümchi.* New York: W. W. Norton, 1999.

Berenson, Kathryn. *Quilts of Provence.* New York: Henry Holt, 1996.

Brédif, Josette. *Printed French Fabrics: Toiles de Jouy.* New York: Rizzoli, 1989.

Burnham, Dorothy K. *Warp & Weft: A Textile Terminology.* Toronto: Royal Ontario Museum, the Hunter Rose Company, 1980.

Calloway, Stephen. *Twentieth-Century Decoration: The Domestic Interior from 1900 to the Present Day.* London: Weidenfeld & Nicolson, 1988.

Carr, William H. A. *The Du Ponts of Delaware: A Fantastic Dynasty.* New York: Dodd, Mead & Company, 1964.

Cooper, Wendy H. *Classical Taste in America: 1800–1840.* Baltimore: Abbeville, 1993.

D'Archimbaut, Nicholas. *Versailles: A New Life Style.* Paris: Editions du Chêne–Hachette Livre, 1999.

A Dictionary of Textile Terms. Danville, VA: Dan River, 1971.

Elliot, Inger McCabe. *Batik: Fabled Cloth of Java.* New York: Clarkson N. Potter, 1984.

Fitzgibbon, Kate, and Andrew Hale. *Ikat: Silks of Central Asia.* London: Laurence King Publishing in association with Alan Marcuson, 1997.

Fowler, John Beresford, and John Cornforth. *English Decoration in the 18th Century.* Princeton, NJ: Pyne Press, 1974.

Garfield, Simon. *Mauve: How One Man Invented a Color That Changed the World.* New York: W. W. Norton & Co., 2001.

Gillow, Barry. *Traditional Indonesian Textiles.* London: Thames and Hudson, 1992.

Honour, Hugh. *Chinoiserie: The Vision of Cathay.* London: John Murray, 1961.

Hurt, Jethro Meriwether, ed. *Old Westbury Gardens: A History and a Guide.* New York: Old Westbury.

Jacobsen, Dawn. *Chinoiserie.* London: Phaidon, 1993.

Levin, Jay. *The Inn at Little Washington: An Insider's Look at the Famed Restaurant and Its Cuisine.* New York: Lebhar-Friedman Books, 2000.

Montgomery, Florence M. *Textiles in America, 1650–1870.* New York: W. W. Norton, 1984.

Nylander, Jane C. *Fabrics for Historic Buildings,* rev. ed. Washington, D.C.: Preservation Press, National Trust for Historic Preservation, 1990.

Nylander, Richard C. *Wallpapers for Historic Buildings,* rev. ed. Washington, D.C.: Preservation Press, National Trust for Historic Preservation, 1992.

Phillips, Betty Lou. *French Influences.* Salt Lake City: Gibbs-Smith, 2001.

Singh, Martand. *Treasures of Indian Textiles.* Bombay: Marge Publications, 1980.

Straeten, Judy. *Toiles de Jouy.* Salt Lake City: Gibbs-Smith, 2003.

Stritzler-Levine, Nina, ed. *Josef Frank: Architect and Designer.* New Haven, CT: Yale University Press, 1996.

Thornton, Peter. *Authentic Decor: The Domestic Interior, 1620–1920.* London: Weidenfeld & Nicolson, 1984.

Wall, Charles C., Christine Meadows, John H. Rhodehamel, and Ellen McCalister Clark. *Mount Vernon: A Handbook.* Ed., Catherine Fallen. Mount Vernon, VA: The Mount Vernon Ladies Association, 1985.

Wingate, Dr. Isobel B. *Fairchild's Dictionary of Textiles,* 6th ed. New York: Fairchild Publications, 1979.

Pamphlets and Periodicals

Abramovitch, Ingrid. "Hats Off!" *House & Garden* (November 2001): 122–31.

Berman, Helene. "East Meets West Indies: A Remarkable Renovation," *Vero Home & Design* 2, no. 2 (2001): 19–24.

Bjennes, Sigrid Hoble. "En ny sommer," *Interior Magasinet 4* (August/September 2003): 23–30.

Boodro, Michael. "All the Trimmings," *House Beautiful* (December 2002): 114–19.

Colman, David. "A Chameleon Shakes the Design World," *New York Times*, October 24, 2002.

Dunlop, Beth. "Grand Tour," *House & Garden* (December 2003): 106–15.

Dunne, Patrick. "A Creole Carol," *House Beautiful* (December 2002): 84–93.

Ennis, Michael. "Ukrainian Jewel Box," *Architectural Digest* (August 2003): 160–65.

Floriani, Elsie M. "Edwardian Influences," *California Home & Design: The Magazine of Design* (October 2002): 116.

Furio, Joanne. "The Whole Nine Yards," *The Journal News* (June 8, 2002): 1E–2E.

Hayes, Christine, ed. "Eastern Delight," *25 Beautiful Homes.* (Summer 2002/3): 98–100.

Konicus, Jura. "More Practical than Posh," *Washington Post,* May 15, 2003.

Lefferts, E. L. "He Colors Rarefied Worlds," *Housatonic Home* (November 2003): 9–10.

Macomber, Paul W. "Double Vision," *Indonesian Tatler* (August 2003): 10–12.

Maison Madame Figaro (October 2003): 112–15.

Maskoutsas, Elaine. "High Notes: Tip-Top Details Add Impact to Valences that Naturally Draw the Eye High," *Window & Wall Ideas* (Summer 2001): 90–97.

Pacheco, Patrick. "A Capital Christmas," *House Beautiful* (December 2002): 120–27.

Phillips, Ian. "The Gilles Factor," *House & Garden* (November 2001): 172–78.

Pochoda, Elizabeth. "Whitman Sampler: In Camden, The Ordinary House of an Extraordinary Poet Is Lovingly Restored," *House & Garden* (April 2000): 142–43.

Porter, Pamela S. "Five Star Dining," *Beautiful Interiors* (2002): 60–61.

Reif, Rita. "Where the Silk Road Took a Detour," *New York Times,* March 22, 1998.

Seebohm, Caroline. "Balancing Act," *Victoria* (November 2001): 90–93.

Smith, Dinitia. "An Estate Lives On, Thanks to Apples," *New York Times,* November 1, 2001.

Acknowledgments

Without the input of the many talented designers who submitted their work, this book would not exist. Our biggest thanks go to them. Our most agonizing maoments were spent having to reject many photographs for technical reasons and due to a limit on illustrations.

Our thanks go to all those in the corporate offices in North White Plains who answered questions and offered help. A special thanks to Chairman Thomas P. Peardon and his wife, Eveline, who allowed their house in Bayeux, France, to be photographed; and to their son, Olivier, and his wife, Susannah, for allowing photography in their apartment in Paris.

Brunschwig & Fils' president, Patrick Mongiello, kindly read through and made improvements on the text covering the all-important business operation of the company. His assistant Leslie Zedlovich sent information through the magic of e-mail. Tom Marshall was always full of enthusiasm for his work despite his busy schedule; Lewis Paul shared his thoughts about the design process.

In New York we were in communication with the Studio and Archive on the eleventh floor of the Decoration and Design Building. Albert Sardelli and his gang at the Studio were always helpful and alert, as was Dorothy Magnani; Judy Straeten in the Archive provided slides and a fund of information; Robert Raymond made wise comments as he looked over text, and Stephen Dahlquist garnered Brunschwig-generated photographs and needed information; and in the final push, Delores Napier was a pillar of strength.

We thank the New York showroom personnel on the twelfth floor for their help in identifying fabrics, wallpapers, furniture, and trimmings in submitted photographs—some of these materials had been discontinued but were still remembered (and often about to be reintroduced).

Our thanks go to all of Brunschwig's showroom managers, who provided names of clients along with great enthusiasm for the book project, and to the photographers whose work is shown here.

As with *Brunschwig & Fils Style,* we imported Alex McLean from Paris, where he now lives, to work on specific photographs in the East Coast area. In the course of our photographic shoots, the following offered help and hospitality: at Clifton House: Nelson Bolton, Stiles Colwell, Diane Wheaton, and Chris Wilson; at the Inn at Little Washington: Patrick O'Connell and Rachel Hayter; at Old Westbury Gardens: Margaret (Peggie) Boegner, Paul Hunchak, and Patricia Speciner.

Others we'd like to thank include Carol Bruce at SPNEA, Mel Marchand at Bob Vila's BVTV, and Mary Roca in Versailles.

Thanks are very much due to Chippy's agent, Angela Miller, who worked with Bulfinch Press to make the book possible. To all those at Bulfinch Press, we would like to thank especially Jill Cohen, Karen Murgolo, our editor, Betty Wong, production manager Denise LaCongo and our designer, Joel Avirom.

Thanks as always are overdue to both our spouses. Albert (Doug) Douglas, Murray's cheerful and hospitable husband, was especially generous in letting us photograph in Chatham, New York, when he would probably have much preferred a relaxing weekend! And thanks to Chippy's husband, decorator Keith Irvine, plus daughters Emma LoMagno and Jassy Irvine and a growing array of cats, for putting put up with our distraction and absences.

Illustration Credits

We have made every effort to give credit to the photographers whose work has been included in this book. Our sincere apologies to any whom we have been unable to track down.

p. ii (l to r): courtesy of the Ritz Hotel, Madrid; Patrick Reynolds; p. iii (l to r): D. Soyer /Mise; Eric Victor; p. v: courtesy Lill Reid; p. vi: Alex McLean; p. viii: Murray Douglas; pp. x–2: Judy Straeten; p. 5: Barry Halkin; p. 6: Peter Vitale; p. 8: Eric Roth; p. 9: Alex McLean; p. 11: Judy Straeten; p. 14: Alex McLean; p. 15: Craig Dugan at Hedrick Blessing; p. 17: Pieter Estersohn; p. 18: Dennis Krukowski; p. 20: courtesy Christy Martin for Studio Encanto; p. 22: Alex McLean; p. 23: Henry Stindt; p. 25: Murray Douglas; p. 26: Ross Chapple; p. 27: Terry Sweeney; p. 28: Judy Straeten; pp. 30–31: Alex McLean; p. 32: courtesy of the Mount Vernon Ladies' Association; p. 33: Hal Conroy, courtesy of Gunston Hall Board of Regents; p. 34: Judy Straeten; p. 35: Judy Straeten, courtesy Hamot; p. 36 (l): Chipper Hatter of Hatter Photographics; (b): Jeff Garland; pp. 37–39: Alex McLean; p. 40: Gordon Beall; p. 41: Henry Stindt; p. 42: Jules, courtesy of Cody & Wolff; p. 44: Murray Douglas; p. 47: Judy Straeten; pp. 49–53: Alex McLean; p. 54: Antony Cotsifas; p. 55: Alex McLean; p. 57 (t): Mel Marchand; (b): Alex McLean; p. 58: Alex McLean; p. 60: courtesy of the Mount Vernon Ladies' Association; p. 63: Robert C. Lautman, courtesy of the Mount Vernon Ladies' Association; p. 64 (b): Judy Straeten; (r): Erik Kvalsvik, © White House Historical Association; p. 67: Bruce White, © White House Historical Association; p. 70: courtesy Lill Reid; pp. 72–73:

William Cummings; p. 75: Pieter Estersohn; p. 76: David Shilling; p. 78 (b): courtesy of Irvine & Fleming; (r): Russell Abraham; p. 81 (t): Barney Taxel & Co.; (b): courtesy Miller and Clarke Interiors; p. 82: Kim Sargent; p. 84: courtesy Lill Reid; p. 85: Aaron Usher; p. 86: Antony Cotsifas; p. 88 (l): Mark Sinclair; (r): Peter Jaquith; p. 90: David Marlow Studio; p. 92 (l): Alex McLean; (r): Carolyn McGinty; p. 94: Murray Douglas; p. 95: Alex McLean; p. 96: Steve Hogben; p. 97 (t): Alex McLean; (b): Sheila Kotur; p. 98: Roger Wade Studio; p. 99: Murray Douglas; pp. 100–101: Peter Vitale, courtesy of *Veranda* magazine; p. 102: Jim Maguire; p. 103: Eric Roth; p. 104 (a): Paul Schlismann; (r): Jeffrey A. Rycus of Rycus Associates Photography; pp. 106–108: Murray Douglas; pp. 110–115: Alex McLean; p. 116 (b): Dries Van den Brande; (r): Stuart McIntyre; p. 118: Brian Harrison of Kudos; p. 119 (t): Cristina Rhodes; (b): José Luis Pérez; p. 120: Shozo and Ysuko Iida; p. 121: Murray Douglas; p. 122: Phillip Ennis; pp. 124–125: Gloria Zinnermann; p. 126: courtesy of Marlene Tablujan; p. 127: Gerard Warrener of Digital Photography in House; p. 128: courtesy Stuart Rattle; p. 130: Simon Kenny; p. 131: Gerard Warrener of Digital Photography in House; p. 132: Sharyn Cairns, Cairns Photography; p. 133 (t): Eric Victor; (b): Patrick Reynolds; p. 134: courtesy of the Ritz Hotel, Madrid; p. 137: Murray Douglas; pp. 138–141: Alex McLean; p. 143: Paul Whicheloe; pp. 144–145: Gordon Beall; pp. 146–149: Christopher Barrett, © Hendrich Blessing; p. 150 (a): courtesy Greg Natale; (r): Melabee M. Miller; p. 154: Daniel Eifert; p. 157: Kelly Bugden; p. 158: Peter Jaquith;

p. 160: David Duncan Livingston; p. 161 (t): Dick Dickinson; (b): Eric Roth; p. 162: Michael Moran; p. 163 (r): Nick Gargala; (b): Tim Murphy of Photo Imagery; p. 164 (a): Pat Shanklin; (r): Peter Margonelli; p. 166: Ross Chapple; p. 167: Janet Mesic Mackie; p. 168: Greg Premru; p. 169: Robert Benson; pp. 170–172 (t): Alex McLean; p. 172 (b): Judy Straeten; pp. 173–176 (t): Alex McLean; (b): Murray Douglas; p. 177: Alex McLean; p. 178: Murray Douglas; p. 179: Chipper Hatter of Hatter Photographics; p. 180 (t): David Van Scott; (b): Alex McLean; p. 181: Alex McLean; pp. 182–185: Maison Madame Figaro; p. 186: Daniel Shanken; p. 187: David Shilling; p. 188: Murray Douglas; p. 190: Olson Photographics; p. 191: Peter Jaquith; p. 192: Eric Roth; p. 193: Sam Gray; p. 194 (t): Joseph O. Weber; (b): Michael Forester; p. 195: Carolyn McGinty; p. 196: Judy Straeten; p. 197: Antony Cotsifas; p. 198: courtesy of Irvine & Fleming; p. 200: Alex McLean; p. 201: Melabee Miller; p. 202: Jason Jung; p. 203: courtesy Stuart Rattle; p. 204: Randl Bye; p. 205 (l to r): Hub Wilson, Frederick Loney III; p. 206: Alex McLean; p. 208: courtesy of Brunschwig & Fils; pp. 209–210: Alex McLean; p.211: James Grant; p. 212 (t): courtesy of Brunschwig & Fils; (c): Hiroski Takama; (b): D. Soyer / Mise; p. 213: Alex McLean; p. 214: Judy Straeten; p. 215: Alex McLean; p. 216 (t): Judy Straeten; (b): Michael Priest; p. 217 (t): Alex McLean; (b): Michael Luppino of Starving Artist's Productions; p. 218: Alex McLean; p. 219: Feliciano; p. 221 (t): courtesy Brunschwig & Fils; (b): Judy Straeten; p. 223: Alex McLean; p. 246: Alex McLean

Index